Drupal 7 First Look

Learn the new features of Drupal 7, how they work and how they will impact you

Mark Noble

PUBLISHING

BIRMINGHAM - MUMBAI

Drupal 7 First Look

First published: November 2010

Production Reference: 1171110

Published by Packt Publishing Ltd.
32 Lincoln Road
Olton
Birmingham, B27 6PA, UK.

ISBN 978-1-849511-22-3

www.packtpub.com

Cover Image by Vinayak Chittar (vinayak.chittar@gmail.com)

Credits

Author
Mark Noble

Reviewer
Maurice Green

Acquisition Editor
Douglas Paterson

Development Editors
Rakesh Shejwal

Swapna Verlekar

Technical Editors
Chris Rodrigues

Ajay Shanker

Indexer
Rekha Nair

Editorial Team Leader
Aanchal Kumar

Project Team Leader
Ashwin Shetty

Project Coordinator
Ashwin Shetty

Proofreader
Stephen Silk

Graphics
Nilesh Mohite

Production Coordinator
Adline Swetha Jesuthas

Cover Work
Adline Swetha Jesuthas

About the Author

Mark Noble has worked in software development and website design for nearly 15 years in a variety of capacities including development, quality assurance, and management. He has worked in a variety of industries including architecture, engineering, library automation, telecommunication, and more. He takes pride in developing software and websites to make businesses run more effectively and delights in helping users to get their jobs done more easily.

Mark owns and operates Turning Leaf Tech, LLC (`http://www.turningleaftech.com`) — a company dedicated to building high-quality web-based solutions for businesses. Projects include both Drupal-based projects and non-Drupal-based sites and solutions. Work ranges from complete site design and implementation to upgrading sites, and building new features to existing sites.

When he isn't behind a computer, Mark enjoys playing with his family, photography, hiking, and traveling.

I would like to thank my family for their support during the writing of this book. You are all amazing, and I love you very much. I would also like to thank the Drupal community for putting out such a fantastic open source application. Without you, books like this would not be possible.

About the Reviewer

Maurice Green began his love affair with computers in 1963 as a graduate student in biochemistry using Fortran and punch cards. Retiring after a 40-year career as a medical laboratory director specializing in automated laboratory instrumentation and information systems and an IT manager in the Department of Medicine at Stanford University, he turned his attention to photography and web design. He is currently the president of the Silicon Valley Computer Society and leads the Digital Imaging and Web Design special interest groups. Maury is the developer and webmaster for the Silicon Valley User Group Alliance website, www.svuga.org. He presented several talks at the Design 4 Drupal conference at Stanford.

Table of Contents

Preface

Welcome to Drupal 7, the next generation of the popular Open Source content management system.

If you are new to Drupal, you will find Drupal 7 to be easy to use, yet extremely powerful. Over the course of this book we will work our way through the most important features of Drupal 7, so you can begin to gain familiarity with Drupal.

For those of you who used Drupal 6 or an earlier version of Drupal, you will find many new enhancements that are designed to make your day-to-day administration tasks easier as well as giving you additional power to extend Drupal to meet the needs of even the most advanced sites. We will spend much of the book discussing the new features of Drupal 7 as well as how Drupal 7 differs from Drupal 6, so you can upgrade your existing sites to the new platform and take advantage of all that Drupal 7 has to offer.

What this book covers

Chapter 1, What's New In Drupal 7?, introduces the reader to the important changes and new features of Drupal 7. It also gives a brief account of the functionality that has been removed entirely, moved into a contributed module, or removed in favor of existing contributed functionality.

Chapter 2, Installation and Upgrades, deals with installing Drupal 7 and upgrading your Drupal 6 site to Drupal 7. It also covers setting up custom installation profiles, so you can install multiple sites using the same basic configuration.

Chapter 3, Site Building with Drupal 7, shows you how to create custom content types with custom fields, add content to your site, translate your content, and leverage all of the new Drupal 7 functionality. It also looks at changes to the Drupal 7 content management system.

Chapter 4, Drupal 7 Administration, looks into changes that have been made to the Administration interface in Drupal 7. It covers information about the new functionality that has been added to Drupal 7 and areas where configuration options have been moved or renamed from Drupal 6 to Drupal 7.

Chapter 5, Drupal 7 for Themers, walks through all of the major changes to the Drupal theme system that were introduced in Drupal 7. It looks at changes to the template files, JavaScript, CSS, and API. It also shows how to upgrade an existing Drupal 6 theme to Drupal 7.

Chapter 6, Drupal 7 Database Changes, deals with the changes to the database abstraction layer of the Drupal API. It introduces the reader to the DBTNG layer.

Chapter 7, Drupal 7 for Developers, looks at the API in terms of upgrading your existing modules and site code to Drupal 7. It also discusses changes related to the Drupal API including changes to the core system, menu system, Form API, and file uploads.

Appendix, Post Publication Changes, because this book was written before the final release of Drupal 7 (much of it was initially written based on early Alpha and Beta versions of the software) some screenshots and descriptions have evolved as Drupal has progressed to its final release. This Appendix will describe any areas that changed after publication. The Appendix is not part of this book but available online at www.packtpub.com for free download.

What you need for this book

Drupal 7 requires PHP 5.2.0 or later to run the Drupal code. You will also need one of the following databases to run Drupal 7:

- MySQL version 5.0 or later
- PostgreSQL 8.3 or later
- SQLite 3.4.2 or later

As always, you can use either Apache HTTP or Microsoft IIS for a web server, but Apache is recommended for best performance and community support.

Who this book is for

Drupal 7 First Look is written for site administrators, themers, and developers who have some experience with Drupal 6 (or even Drupal 5) and want to upgrade their sites, themes, or modules to Drupal 7 or just learn more about Drupal 7. No programming experience is required, but several code examples are covered for readers that want more in-depth information about building themes and modules.

Conventions

In this book, you will find a number of styles of text that distinguish between different kinds of information. Here are some examples of these styles, and an explanation of their meaning.

Code words in text are shown as follows: "You can increase the available memory and execution time in your `php.ini` file".

A block of code is set as follows:

```
dependencies[] = block
dependencies[] = color
dependencies[] = comment
dependencies[] = dashboard
...
```

Any command-line input or output is written as follows:

```
php install.site.php
```

New terms and **important words** are shown in bold. Words that you see on the screen, in menus or dialog boxes for example, appear in the text like this: "Find the latest official release of Drupal 7 and click on the **Download** link".

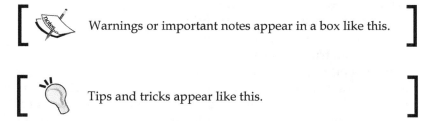

Warnings or important notes appear in a box like this.

Tips and tricks appear like this.

Reader feedback

Feedback from our readers is always welcome. Let us know what you think about this book—what you liked or may have disliked. Reader feedback is important for us to develop titles that you really get the most out of.

To send us general feedback, simply send an e-mail to feedback@packtpub.com, and mention the book title via the subject of your message.

If there is a book that you need and would like to see us publish, please send us a note in the **SUGGEST A TITLE** form on www.packtpub.com or e-mail suggest@packtpub.com.

If there is a topic that you have expertise in and you are interested in either writing or contributing to a book, see our author guide on www.packtpub.com/authors.

Customer support

Now that you are the proud owner of a Packt book, we have a number of things to help you to get the most from your purchase.

Downloading the example code for this book

You can download the example code files for all Packt books you have purchased from your account at http://www.PacktPub.com. If you purchased this book elsewhere, you can visit http://www.PacktPub.com/support and register to have the files e-mailed directly to you.

Errata

Although we have taken every care to ensure the accuracy of our content, mistakes do happen. If you find a mistake in one of our books—maybe a mistake in the text or the code—we would be grateful if you would report this to us. By doing so, you can save other readers from frustration and help us improve subsequent versions of this book. If you find any errata, please report them by visiting http://www.packtpub.com/support, selecting your book, clicking on the **errata submission form** link, and entering the details of your errata. Once your errata are verified, your submission will be accepted and the errata will be uploaded on our website, or added to any list of existing errata, under the Errata section of that title. Any existing errata can be viewed by selecting your title from http://www.packtpub.com/support.

Piracy

Piracy of copyright material on the Internet is an ongoing problem across all media. At Packt, we take the protection of our copyright and licenses very seriously. If you come across any illegal copies of our works, in any form, on the Internet, please provide us with the location address or website name immediately so that we can pursue a remedy.

Please contact us at copyright@packtpub.com with a link to the suspected pirated material.

We appreciate your help in protecting our authors, and our ability to bring you valuable content.

Questions

You can contact us at questions@packtpub.com if you are having a problem with any aspect of the book, and we will do our best to address it.

What's New In Drupal 7?

It's finally here! After nearly three years of development, Drupal 7 is now available for use on production sites! Drupal 7 is loaded with tons of great new features aimed at novice as well as experienced website administrators.

If you have been reluctant to try Drupal because you thought the learning curve would be too difficult or that it would be hard to install Drupal, you will be pleased to know that the installation process has been streamlined and the administration interface has been made more usable and easier to learn. Several commonly-used features have now been included into the base Drupal installation, so they are easily available to everyone.

Power users of Drupal will also rejoice at new time-saving improvements to make it easier to build custom modules and themes. Experienced users will also benefit from improved organization in the new administration interface as well as other new, built-in features included in Drupal 7.

Goals of Drupal 7

When development on Drupal 7 first started, there were several goals that Dries Buytaert, the founder of Drupal, laid out. They are as follows:

- **Better media handling**: Make it easier to add images, Flash, Flex, and so on to websites built with Drupal.

- **Custom content types in core**: Integrate portions of the CCK module into core to allow site administrators to apply this functionality more easily.

- **WYSIWYG editor**: Incorporate a **What You See Is What You Get** HTML editor into core, so editors can add formatted text to their sites more easily.

- **Better performance and scalability**: Make sites built on Drupal leaner and faster to load, improve performance for users that are logged into the site, and make it easier for Drupal to be used on sites that get lots of traffic.

- **Better tools to structure/organize content**: Make it easier to create a meaningful site structure to hold all content in a way that makes sense for both administrators and visitors.

- **Basic Views-like module**: Incorporate portions of the Views module to make it easier for site administrators to present site content in different, interesting ways to visitors.

- **Automatic upgrade functionality**: Allow site administrators to download and install updates to Drupal, contributed modules, and contributed themes without needing to download and unpack tarballs and then manually deploy them to a site, making Drupal as easy to upgrade as your operating system.

- **Improved node access system**: Improve control and permissions for who can access which nodes and what they can do to each node.

- **Better internal APIs**: Make it easier to maintain Drupal and add custom modules for site-specific functionality.

- **Better external APIs**: Make it easier to import data into a site and export data from a site. Improve functionality allowing administrators to consume and expose web services.

- **Usability**: Reduce the learning curve for new users and make common tasks faster and easier to get to for experienced users.

These primary goals were taken from a poll conducted on the official Drupal website (`http://drupal.org`), and are reflective of the opinions of over a thousand people in the Drupal community. The goals for Drupal 7 also reflect a stated plan of focusing more on the end user and larger websites.

Key new features in Drupal 7

As with any project, not all of the initial goals were completed and several additional features were incorporated that weren't part of the initial plan. Let's look at the key functionality that did make it into Drupal 7.

Improved installation

The first thing you will notice if you are installing Drupal 7 for the first time is the new installation routine. The new routine is designed to make it easier for new Drupal users to set up Drupal. The new installation offers two types of install—the regular installation and a minimal installation.

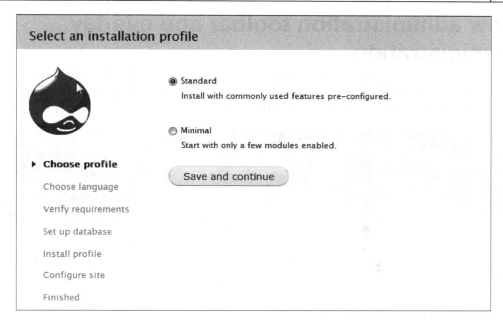

The **Minimal** installation is similar to previous versions. The new **Standard** installation automatically enables commonly-used functionality during the installation to save time after setup. The installation also automatically performs common startup tasks, like building an administrator role. Finally, the new installation system also allows for command-line installation of Drupal.

We will explore installation and updating in more detail in Chapter 5.

New administration toolbar and overlay administration

After installing or upgrading to Drupal 7 you will immediately notice the new administration toolbar (shown in the following screenshot) that appears on all pages if you have the permission to administer the site:

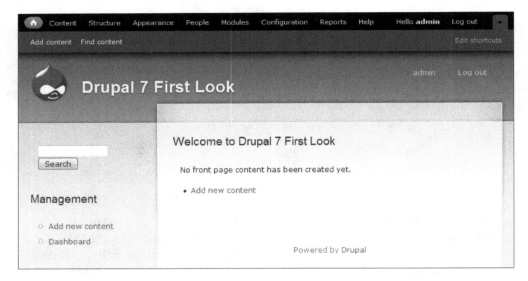

The toolbar groups commonly used tasks together making it easier for new administrators to learn how to configure Drupal and making it quicker for experienced administrators to get to commonly-used functionality.

Selecting an option from the toolbar will open a new overlay window, so you can change configuration options without losing your place on the site.

An example of the overlay panel is shown as follows:

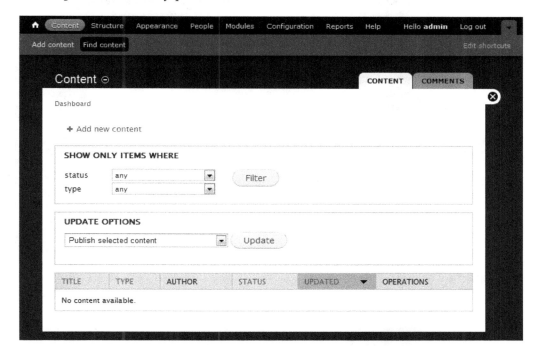

 Power users can disable use of the overlay window either by removing permission to use the overlay panel or disabling the overlay panel.

We will review the dashboard and new administration interface in detail in Chapter 3.

Improved interface for creating content

A big, but welcome, change for editors is the redesigned and updated interface to create and edit content. A sample of the interface is shown in the following screenshot:

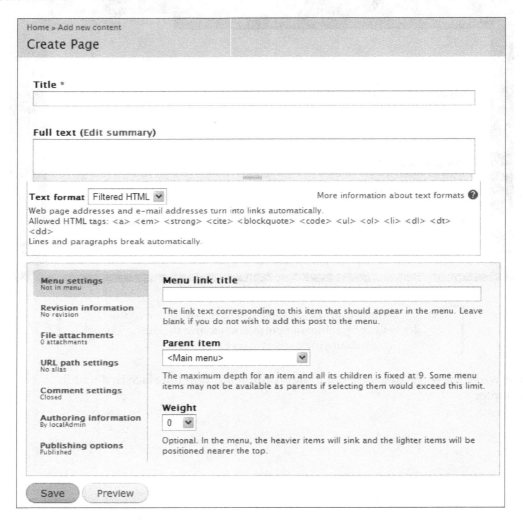

The redesigned screen makes it easier to quickly navigate to specific sections within the content. It is also a more intuitive interface. We will dive into creating content in depth in Chapter 2.

Improved interface for creating new content types

In Chapter 2, we will also explore the new, more intuitive, interface for building content types, which is shown in the following screenshot:

The interface for creating content types has been redesigned to keep all of the options in a smaller space so navigation is easier and all information can be quickly accessed.

New Field API

A welcome sight to many Drupal administrators and editors is the inclusion of the
Field API in Drupal core.

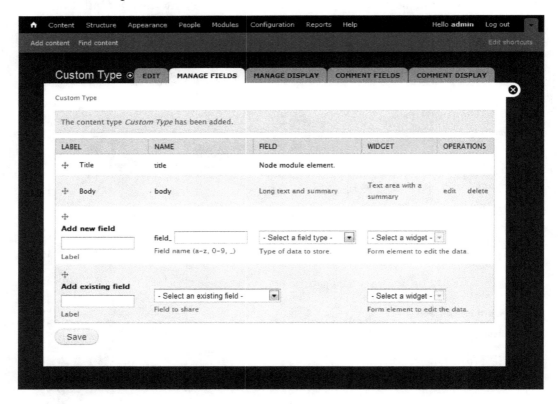

The Field API was built from the Drupal 6 CCK (Content Construction Kit)
contributed module. It allows site administrators to add additional attributes to a
node type. A field can have a variety of different types and be displayed in many
different widgets (user interface elements). The Field API also supports translatable
fields to allow for multi-lingual sites. We will explore the Field API in detail in
Chapter 2.

Additional support for files and images

Building on the new Field API, Drupal 7 offers two new types of fields that will be useful on many sites – the file field and the image field. The file field allows editors and users with proper permission to upload files and attach them to nodes. The file field also gives administrators a wide range of configuration options to control the type and size of files that can be added, where the files are stored, and how the files are displayed within the node.

The image field builds on the file field to add functionality specifically needed for images. Image fields can be added to content types and configured much like any other field.

After adding an image field to a content type, you can control how the resulting image is displayed on the site through a series of simple configuration options on the field. Users with proper permissions can upload images directly to the site and Drupal will take care of resizing the images to generate thumbnails for proper display on your site. Drupal 7 also has new functionality to allow rotating and applying various other effects to images.

We will explore all of the new file and image features in Chapter 2.

Improved filter system

Filters allow administrators to control what can be inserted into text fields. For example, an administrator can only allow basic formatting like bolding and italicizing text to be inserted into content. Or, they can allow more advanced functionality like linking to images and inserting tables. An administrator can even allow PHP to be inserted within a text field. Drupal 7 renames Input Filters to Text Formats and adds some additional capabilities including the ability to assign text formats to different roles using the permission system. We will explore text formats more in Chapter 2.

Added context information to messages during translation

Translators and administrators of multi-language sites will love the new contextual information for messages. In prior versions of Drupal, one of the issues translators faced was messages that were used in different situations and therefore had different meanings. The problem was worse with short messages consisting of only a few words because the meaning could be more easily confused. Drupal 7 adds an optional context for the translation to allow developers and themers to make translatable strings less ambiguous. Because the context information is optional, performance is not negatively impacted. We will touch on translations throughout the book as appropriate, but most of the information on translations will be found in Chapters 2 and 3.

Built-in automated cron functionality

Many site administrators will be pleased to see the inclusion of a new cron system for Drupal that does not rely on running cron from the Unix cron system. In previous versions, this could be one of the most confusing and difficult configuration steps for a new site administrator. Now, it is a simple matter of selecting how often you want cron to run. The mechanism used is similar to the one used by `poormanscron` except that it runs from an AJAX request rather than delaying the response time of the page triggering cron. We will explore the new cron functionality more in Chapter 3.

Improved security

Security is always important to site administrators and Drupal 7 will please security-conscious administrators with several important new security enhancements including:

- Cron is now secure and requires a key to be run from remote sites. This can help prevent denial of service attacks and overloading the server processor
- Improved password protection including a new pluggable password system and stronger password hashing
- Limiting invalid login attempts to prevent brute force attacks
- Improved IP address blocking

Chapter 3 will cover these and many more security changes in detail.

Added a new plugin manager

While we talk about security and improvements to administration in Chapter 3, we will also cover the brand new plugin manager. The plugin manager allows automatic updates of your Drupal installation. The plugin manager will automatically download the appropriate updates from the Drupal website via FTP and place the downloaded packages on your site in the correct locations. The module has appropriate permissions to ensure that the update process is carefully controlled so the administrator knows exactly what is occurring.

Added the Seven theme for administration

A common complaint of Drupal administrators in previous versions was the look of the administration interface and that it could be difficult to tell when you were in the administration interface, since it used the same theme as regular content by default. To fix this, Drupal 7 has added a new administration theme called the Seven theme that is enabled by default.

The Seven theme uses a single column layout with muted colors and is an obvious contrast to the default blue colors of the default user themes. The following are a couple of samples showing how it appears on different pages (with the overlay disabled):

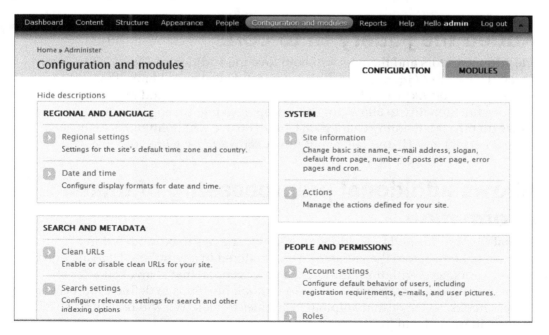

The previous view displays information in a single main column with each section of settings displayed in a smaller block in two columns. The next view shows a basic list of links:

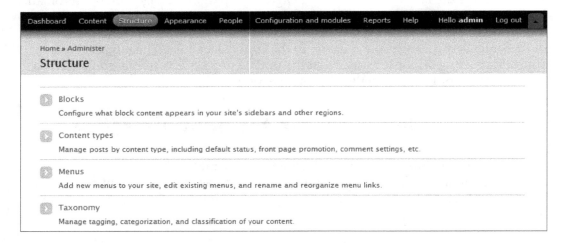

The Garland theme is still used by default when viewing content. Drupal 7 preserves the ability to modify the administration theme to be any theme you want or to set the administration theme to always be the default site theme.

Added the jQuery UI to core

Site administrators and themers will both love the addition of jQuery UI to core. jQuery UI (http://jqueryui.com) is a powerful JavaScript library that includes common controls like calendars, progress bars, tabs, sliders, and more. It also includes functionality to allow drag and drop, resizing, sorting, selection, and more. As we go through theming changes in Chapter 6, we will point out areas where Drupal uses jQuery UI and talk about how to add jQuery UI to your site.

Allows additional preprocessing of themed information

Drupal 6 added the ability to add and modify variables to be rendered in a preprocess hook before the variables were rendered in a template. This functionality has been enhanced with the addition of a process hook that is invoked after all preprocessing is done. Drupal 7 also allows hook functions to define preprocess and process hooks, so they can manipulate variables as well. We will review these API changes in more detail in Chapter 6.

Added the New Stark theme

Several core Drupal 6 themes, which were not widely used and served mainly as examples, were removed in favor of the new Stark theme that is designed to make it easier to learn how to build a custom theme. The Stark theme should not be used on its own since it is not very attractive. However, it serves as a reference point for understanding the default HTML that Drupal emits as well as the default styling that Drupal provides. This information can be used to help identify problems with custom themes or to identify conflicts with modules that have been enabled. We will use the Stark theme in Chapter 6 as we review changes to Drupal's default themes and styles.

Rewritten database layer (DBTNG)

Arguably the biggest change in Drupal 7, at least for developers, is the new database layer, also called **DBTNG** (short for **Database Layer: The Next Generation**). DBTNG is a big change for developers since it changes how modules interact with the database. We will explore DBTNG in great detail in Chapter 7, but here are some of the highlights:

- Includes a new database layer built on **PDO (PHP Data Objects)**. PDO provides a consistent lightweight interface for accessing a wide variety of databases including MySQL, PostgreSQL, SQL Server, and Oracle. More information about PDO can be found at: http://www.php.net/pdo.

- Adds a query builder to handle creating SELECT, INSERT, UPDATE, and DELETE statements. The query builder is designed to make accessing the database easier, more extensible, and more secure.

- Provides support for replicating databases in master/slave and master/master configurations.

- Improved support for connecting to multiple databases at a time.

- Support for transactions when using transactional databases, with proper fallback when not connected to a transactional database.

There are many other exciting changes in the DBTNG layer that we will review in more detail later.

Improved node access system

Several changes have been made to the underlying node access system to improve the granularity of permissions, improve security, and make it easier for developers to properly maintain restrictions to nodes.

The first major change is the splitting of the administer nodes permission into two permissions, administer nodes and bypass node access. This allows administrators to give users the ability to administer only nodes to which they normally have access. We will discuss this further in Chapter 4.

The next major change is the ability for custom modules to influence the access to nodes even if they did not define the original access rules for the node. This gives developers more control over the logic needed to control access to information and functionality of the site. We will review these new APIs in Chapter 7.

Another change is a one step function call when using the DBTNG layer that instructs DBTNG to add node access restrictions to the query. This will make setting up proper security restrictions much easier to include and it will be easier to detect potential node access bypasses during code reviews. We will cover this API in more detail in Chapter 7.

Lastly, Drupal 7 adds additional restrictions for who can access unpublished content. We will review this change primarily in Chapter 3, but we will also touch on it in Chapter 7.

Added the Queue API for long-running tasks

Eventually, most websites find a task that takes a long time to perform and can't be optimized enough to be completed before the web browser times out. To take this situation into account, Drupal 7 adds a Queue API to manage long-running tasks. In general, any task that takes more than 30 seconds to a minute would be an excellent candidate for the Queue API. We will walk through the Queue API in Chapter 7.

Added a new test framework

Drupal 7 adds a comprehensive test framework called testing that allows developers and site administrators to run tests against an existing Drupal installation to ensure that it is behaving properly. Developers of custom modules can create their own tests to ensure that their module works properly and that the functionality does not regress when new versions of Drupal are released.

Portions of the test framework were back ported to Drupal 6 as the `SimpleTest` test framework, so you may already have some familiarity with it. We will look into the Test framework in more detail in Chapter 7.

RDF capabilities

A key concept of Web 3.0 sites is the use of Semantic Web technologies that allow sites to provide additional information about the meaning of the content provided within the site. One of these technologies is **RDF (Resource Description Framework)**, which adds metadata to a page to give additional contextual information about the information on the page. Providing RDF information can help search engines and other applications to better understand your content, which may lead to improved search engine positions and more site visitors. Drupal 7 allows RDF information to be attached to entire nodes as well as fields within a node using the RDFa specification.

Unmet goals

Like any major development project, there are always a few things that you would like to implement but couldn't complete for various reasons. For Drupal 7, there were two initial goals that were not completed.

Initially, putting a WYSIWYG editor into Drupal was desired to help content editors to edit their sites more easily. However, this effort was postponed from Drupal 7 due to the lack of a standard WYSIWYG editor that could be included and the need for more design to create a solution that will work for a majority of users. Although there is not a full-fledged WYSIWYG editor in core, a number of changes have been made to core to help future integration efforts. We will review these changes more in Chapters 2 and 3. Much of the work that was done for Drupal 7 is now available in the contributed WYSIWYG module (`http://drupal.org/project/wysiwyg`). We will review the WYSIWYG module in more detail in Chapter 4.

The other main goal that was not realized was the inclusion of Views within Drupal core. This is primarily due to the complexity of Views and determination of whether or not the entire functionality of Views should be included in Drupal 7 or if only a subset of the functionality belonged within Drupal 7. However, several concepts that originated from the Views interface have migrated into Drupal core and the new DBTNG API makes it easier for developers to create complex queries of the Drupal database.

Key changes to Drupal 7

An important attribute of the Drupal development process is the concept that changes need not be backwards compatible with previous major versions. This allows Drupal developers to make changes to the underlying structure of the code making it more robust, easier to maintain, easier to extend, and faster. Sometimes these changes are transparent to site administrators, developers, and themers. In other cases, you may need to make changes to your site, module, or themes to take advantage of this new functionality or make it compatible with the changes.

We will explore these changes in detail in future chapters, but here are some of the major changes that may affect your sites, modules, and themes:

- The footer message and mission statements have been removed and replaced with a simple custom block. Old sites will be upgraded during the installation process if they used the footer message or mission statement.

- A new default region called help has been added in addition to the default regions: header, left, right, content, and footer.

- The content region is now required and the main text of a page is rendered as a block to allow other blocks to appear before it in the content region.

- JavaScript and CSS files for a theme are no longer detected automatically and must be added to your theme's .info file. Similarly, all code files must be identified in a module's .info file. This will help to improve overall performance since Drupal will not need to constantly scan for which files to include.

- The search box no longer needs to be rendered by the theme. It is now part of the block system and can be rendered in any location using standard block functionality.

- The Taxonomy API has been reworked to make it easier to use and to make it more consistent with other APIs. We will cover this in more detail during Chapter 2.

- Several APIs have had parameters added, deleted, or renamed. Some functions have been renamed or removed entirely. We will cover these in detail during Chapter 7.

In addition to these changes, several other modifications have been made to Drupal's core functionality, which we will explore throughout the remainder of this book.

Removed functionality

The developers of Drupal adhere to the principle that simpler is generally better. Therefore some of the functionality that existed in the Drupal 6 core has either been removed entirely, moved into a contributed module, or removed in favor of existing contributed functionality. Here are some of the functionalities that have been removed as well as some suggestions for replacing that functionality if you relied on it in a Drupal 6 site:

- Blocking of IP addresses using ranges has been removed. You can block single IP addresses within Drupal. However, blocking by range should be done at the operating system or firewall level.

- Removed Bluemarine, Chameleon, and Pushbutton themes and made them contributed themes. These can be accessed at:
  - `http://drupal.org/project/bluemarine`
  - `http://drupal.org/project/chameleon`
  - `http://drupal.org/project/pushbutton`

- Removed per-user themes. Users can no longer select which theme they want to use in the default Drupal installation. There are several contributed themes that contain similar functionality and either allow users to change their entire theme or select between various color variations to customize the site.

- Removed the `mime_extension_mapping` variable that allowed files to be remapped to different file types. This can now be done using the `hook_file_mimetype_mapping_alter()` hook.

- The footer message and site mission settings have been removed and can be recreated with a custom block.

- The Blog API module has been removed and replaced with a contributed module. (`http://drupal.org/project/blogapi`). There are also several other contributed modules that perform similar functionality.

- Removed the Ping module that broadcasted a message to other sites when your site was updated. There are several other contributed modules that have similar functionality.

- Removed the Throttle module that disabled site functionality when the site became busy. The Throttle module was removed because it was less effective than other methods (like aggressive caching) at improving performance, and because it was not widely used. Administrators interested in this module should consider using other caching techniques to improve performance.

Contributed modules

One of the major problems when moving from Drupal 5 to Drupal 6 was the slow rate of migration for many of the modules and themes that were contributed to the Drupal project by Drupal community members. If a site relied on a module that had not been updated, they had to delay upgrading their sites, assist in conversion efforts, find an alternative solution, or rebuild the existing functionality themselves. Thankfully, this should not reoccur with migrations from Drupal 6 to Drupal 7. A large number of module maintainers pledged to have full releases of their modules available the day that Drupal 7 is released. This list includes several key modules that are used by many sites.

We will look into some of the contributed modules that have Drupal 7 releases in Chapter 4, with information about changes you may need to make if you are using them in your Drupal 6 site.

Minimum requirements for Drupal 7

Implementing all of these features does require some upgrades to other software on your server. Drupal 7 now requires PHP 5.2.0 or later to run the Drupal code. You will also need one of the following databases to run Drupal 7:

- MySQL version 5.0 or later
- PostgreSQL 8.3 or later
- SQLite 3.4.2 or later

Most hosting companies will already have these installed, but if your server is a little out of date, now is the time to update.

As always, you can use either Apache HTTPD or Microsoft IIS for a web server, but Apache is recommended for best performance and community support.

 Not all contributed modules for Drupal have been verified to work correctly with PHP 5.3. If you want to use PHP 5.3, carefully test all modules for proper compatibility.

Summary

In this chapter, we covered the most important changes and new features of Drupal 7 at a very high level. I hope that we have piqued your interest in Drupal 7 and that you are ready to dive into Drupal 7 in more detail. We will start our in-depth investigation by thoroughly reviewing changes and new functionality related to the content management system of Drupal 7.

2
Installation and Upgrades

Before we start looking at all of the great new features in Drupal 7 in detail, let's walk through the process for installing Drupal 7 and upgrading Drupal 6 sites to Drupal 7. Several aspects of the installation process have changed, including:

- A new installation option that installs commonly-used features by default
- A command-line installation process
- Better support for installation profiles

After we have looked at the installation process, we will move on to upgrading your Drupal 6 website to Drupal 7.

Installing Drupal 7

Drupal's installation process has always been very easy to use, and the Drupal 7 installation makes things even easier.

Before beginning to install Drupal 7, you will need a web server running the Apache HTTPD web server. You can also use IIS on Microsoft Windows, but the Apache server is preferred and you will be able to obtain support from the community more easily if you use the Apache server.

Want to easily install Apache onto a Microsoft Windows machine? Try XAMPP, which is published by Apache Friends. This package includes Apache, MySQL, and PHP with a standard Microsoft Windows installer. You can download XAMPP from `http://www.apachefriends.org/en/xampp.html`. Other options include WAMP (`http://www.wampserver.com/en/`) and MoWeS Portable (`http://www.chsoftware.net/en/mowes/mowesportable/mowes.htm`).

Your server will also need PHP installed on it. Drupal requires at least PHP version 5.2.0. As of this writing, there are some hosts that still do not have PHP 5.2.0 or later installed on their shared hosting accounts, and Red Hat does not include PHP 5.2.0 or later in its default distribution. Check with your host or system administrator before installing Drupal to make sure that the correct version is available.

In addition to the web server and PHP, you will also need a database. MySQL and PostgreSQL are the databases that are most frequently used with Drupal, and of the two, MySQL is much more widely used. That being said, you can use Drupal with many different databases and the new DBTNG database abstraction layer will make it easier to deploy to any database. If you are using MySQL, you will need version 5.0.15 or later installed. If you are using PostgreSQL, you will need PostgreSQL 8.3.0 or later. SQLite is also officially supported for use with Drupal and you will need version 3.4.2 or later.

After you have a server set up with the proper software, you can download Drupal and begin the installation process.

Obtaining Drupal

If you have used previous versions of Drupal, the process for downloading Drupal is the same as always. If you are new to Drupal, you will use the following process:

1. Go to the Drupal project page on Drupal.org: `http://drupal.org/project/drupal`.

2. Find the latest official release of Drupal 7 and click on the **Download** link. The release will be named 7.0 or similar.

3. Your browser will ask whether you want to **download** or **Open** the file. Make sure to download it to your computer.

4. The file you downloaded is a `.tar.gz` file, which is a compressed archive similar to a `.zip` file. You will need to extract the files from this archive onto your computer.

 If your computer doesn't already have a program that can open `.tar.gz` files, try 7-Zip, an open source application that easily handles these files. You can download 7-Zip from `http://www.7-zip.org`.

5. After you have extracted the files, you will need to copy them to your web server's document root.

6. You are now ready to start the installation process. Simply navigate to `http://yoursite.com/install.php`.

Let's step through the installation process in detail now.

Selecting an installation profile

The first step in the installation process is selecting an installation profile. Drupal prompts you with a screen asking for which installation profile you want to use during the installation:

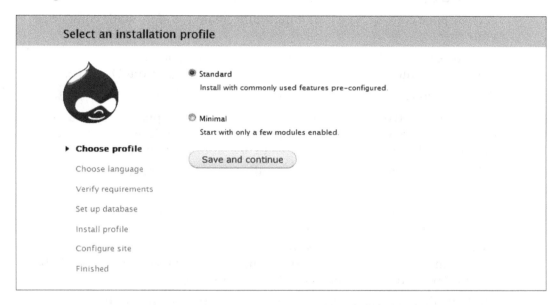

By default, Drupal comes with two installation profiles, the **Standard** profile and the **Minimal** profile. Custom distributions may come with additional profiles. We will discuss creating custom installation profiles at the end of this chapter.

Minimal profile

The **Minimal** profile installs a basic configuration of Drupal with only the required functionality enabled. This profile is even more minimal than the base Drupal 6 installation.

This profile should be used if you are very familiar with setting up Drupal and don't want some of the additional features activated in the **Standard** profile.

Standard profile

The **Standard** Drupal profile installs and activates several commonly-used features to make your Drupal site more useful immediately. These additional features include:

- **Search** form installed on the left sidebar.
- **Powered by Drupal** block enabled in the footer.
- A basic page content type is automatically created to store static content on your site.
- An article content type is automatically created to store time-specific content. The article content type replaces the story content type from Drupal 6.
- Both content types are set up with RDF capabilities.
- User profiles have pictures enabled by default. Profile pictures can have a maximum size of 1024x1024 pixels and be up to 800 KB when they are uploaded. They will be displayed using the thumbnail image style.
- A taxonomy called **Tags** is created to allow easy categorization of content on your site.
- The article content type is enhanced by adding an image field, which allows PNG, GIF, and JPG files to be attached to the article.
- An administrator role is created that has all permissions activated for it. As new modules are activated, the administrator role will automatically be updated with the permissions for the new module.
- The Seven theme is activated for the administration section of the site.

In most cases, you will want to start with the **Standard** installation profile, especially if you are setting up an entirely new site or if you are new to Drupal.

Language selection

The next step in the installation is choosing the language with which you want to install Drupal. By default, Drupal only includes an English installer. If you want to want to install Drupal in another language, you will need to download a translation from Drupal.org. A complete list of translations is available at `http://drupal.org/project/translations`. After you download the translation you want to use, you will need to unpack the translation and copy it to your document folder. The process to unpack and copy the files is similar to the process we used when we unpacked and copied the core Drupal files to your server.

For now, we will continue with the English installation.

Requirements check

Drupal will now check the requirements of your server to ensure that it meets the minimum requirements to run Drupal and to ensure that everything is ready for the installation to proceed.

The requirements check will appear similar to the following:

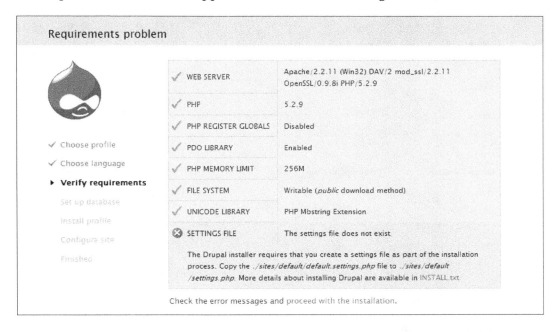

If Drupal does discover any problems, it will give you information about how to correct the problem. In our case, it looks like we forgot to set up our settings file. The settings file tells Drupal which database to connect to as well as the connection information. To create a settings file, navigate to your document root and then navigate to the sites/default folder. Copy the default.settings.php file to settings.php. You do not need to change any of the information within the file.

After you have corrected any problems, click on the **proceed with the installation** link. Drupal will re-evaluate the requirements and let you know if anything else needs to be changed.

This screen has been enhanced in Drupal 7 to provide much more information about your current server settings.

Database configuration

The next step in installing Drupal is configuring the database where Drupal will store the content and configuration information for your site. The functionality of this screen has also been enhanced in Drupal 7.

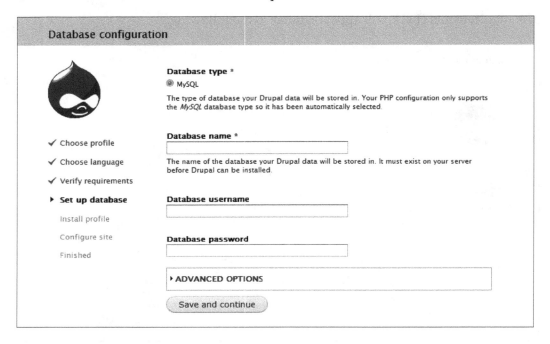

The key difference is that Drupal 7 will automatically check which types of databases are available to you based on your server setup. Then, it will only allow you to select a database which will work.

If you want to run Drupal using a different database server than your web server, you can use the **ADVANCED OPTIONS** link to configure the database server and port. You can also use **ADVANCED OPTIONS** if you are setting up multiple sites within a single database.

For a Standard installation, enter the name of your database as well as the username and password for the database. This functionality remains the same as in Drupal 6.

You will need to create a database outside of the Drupal installation. The actual steps for creating a new database vary depending on your website host. Many hosts have installed phpMyAdmin, which allows you to manage your databases with an easy-to-use web-based interface.

If you use phpMyAdmin to create your database, you will need to log in to phpMyAdmin and create a database. You can create a new database from the home page, which should appear similar to the following screenshot depending on the version of phpMyAdmin you are using:

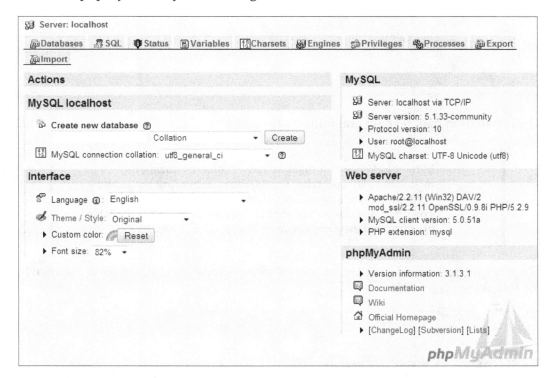

You can create a new user for the database in the **Privileges** tab.

After you have entered your database settings, click on the **Save and continue** button. Drupal will now configure the database and set up your site.

As the installation proceeds, Drupal will display its progress.

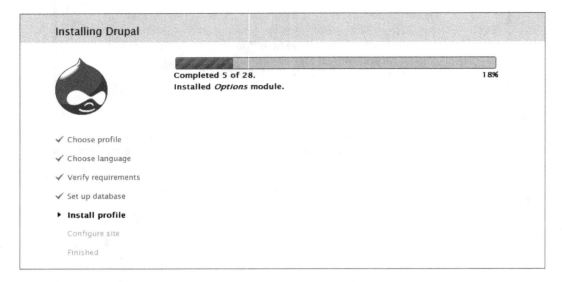

The installation may take several minutes to complete.

In the unlikely event that you have problems during the installation, try emptying the database, increasing the amount of memory available to Drupal, and increasing the maximum execution time for a PHP script. You can increase the available memory and execution time in your php.ini file.

The relevant sections in php.ini to control memory and execution time are shown in the following screenshot:

```
;;;;;;;;;;;;;;;;;;;;
; Resource Limits ;
;;;;;;;;;;;;;;;;;;;;

max_execution_time = 60      ; Maximum execution time of each script, in seconds
max_input_time = 60 ; Maximum amount of time each script may spend parsing request data
memory_limit = 256M         ; Maximum amount of memory a script may consume (16MB)
```

Configure site

After the Standard installation has completed, you will need to configure your site.

The basic configuration starts by asking you for the **SITE INFORMATION** and **SITE MAINTENANCE ACCOUNT** details. The site maintenance account has the ability to change all settings within the site. You should make sure that the **Password** is difficult to guess and that it is stored securely.

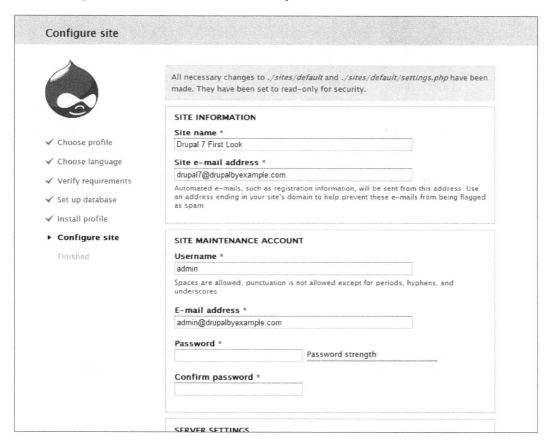

These options are identical to the Drupal 6 settings.

The next set of configuration options allow you to determine which country your site is located in as well as the **Default time zone** for the site:

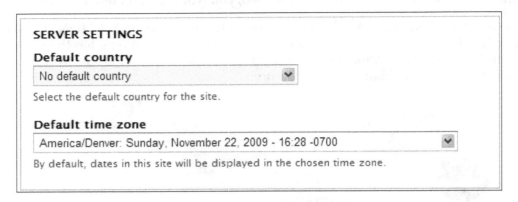

The **Default country** setting is new to Drupal 7 and the **Default time zone** setting has been made easier to understand by adding the name of the time zone.

The final set of configuration options are related to updating your site:

These settings allow you to have Drupal automatically check if any updates are available for Drupal or any contributed modules you have installed. If there are any updates available, you can optionally have Drupal e-mail you so you don't have to constantly check for updates on your own. It is highly recommended that you activate both of these options.

Drupal 6 administrators may have noticed that there is no setting for clean URLs. By default, Drupal 7 will activate clean URLs if your site is capable of using them.

After you have entered the configuration options to your satisfaction, click on the **Save and continue** button to finalize your choices.

After all options have been saved to the database, you will be given a final status screen stating that the installation completed successfully.

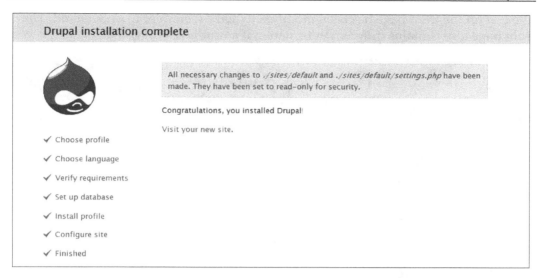

Now that the installation is finished, we can finally navigate to our site by clicking on the **Visit your new site** link.

New home page

The default home page has also been changed from Drupal 6, as shown in the following screenshot:

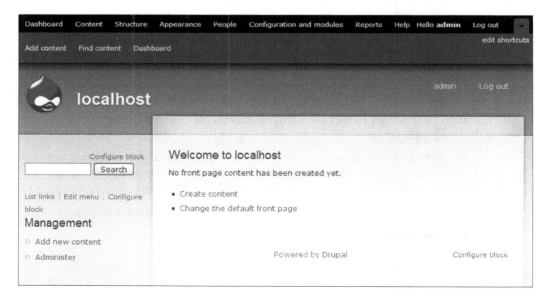

The text on the front page has been modified to make it simpler to understand. The front page also contains different information if a user is not logged in.

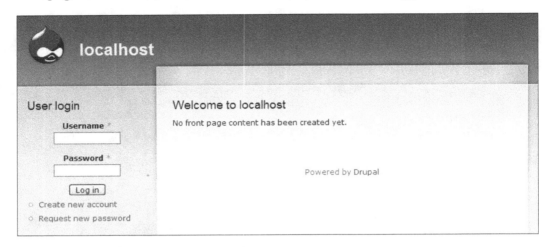

This helps to ensure that unnecessary information is not displayed to site visitors.

Now that we have gone through the entire Standard installation, let's look at some of the more advanced things you can do with the Drupal installer.

Command-line installation

Administrators who manage lots of sites or who prefer to work from the command line will be thrilled with the change to make Drupal installable from the command line. If you want to run the installation from the command line, you will need to use the following procedure:

1. Download Drupal from Drupal.org and copy the files to your server.

2. Create a PHP script to run the Drupal command line using the following procedure:

    i. Create a file called `install.site.php` where `site` is the name of your site. This file should be located in the same directory where your `install.php` file is located (the root directory for your site).

    ii. Open the `install.site.php` file in your favorite file editor.

    iii. Enter the following script:

    ```php
    <?php
    include_once 'install.php';

    $settings = array(
    ```

```
        'parameters' => array(
          'profile' => 'default',
          'locale' => 'en',
        ),
        'forms' => array(
          'install_settings_form' => array(
            'driver' => 'mysql',
            'database' => 'my_db_name',
            'username' => 'my_db_username',
            'password' => 'my_db_password',
          ),
          'install_configure_form' => array(
            'site_name' => 'My site',
            'site_mail' => 'admin@example.com',
            'account' => array(
              'name' => 'admin',
              'mail' => 'admin@example.com',
              'pass' => array(
                'pass1' => 'my_site_password',
                'pass2' => 'my_site_password',
              ),
            ),
            'update_status_module' => array(1 => TRUE),
            'clean_url' => TRUE,
          ),
        ),
      );
      install_drupal($settings);
      ?>
```

This code is used to configure the installation so Drupal knows what values to use during the installation process to properly configure your site as it is created.

iv. Modify the values in the above code snippet to match the needs of the site you want to install. You will need to pay special attention to the database information including the database name, username, and password. You should also modify the administrator's password, site name, and so on to match the desired values for your site.

v. Save the file with all of your changes.

3. Run the `install.site.php` file from the command line using the syntax:
   php install.site.php

4. After the installation completes, you can verify your site and begin configuring it as usual.

5. After completing the installation, you should back up the install file and either remove it from your site completely or remove access to the file for all users since it contains the login information for User 1.

Although this setup is a little more complicated to run initially, it can be a big time saver if you are installing a large number of sites or want to run an unattended installation.

Upgrading from Drupal 6 to Drupal 7

The Drupal upgrade process allows you to update your site from Drupal 6 to Drupal 7 using a simple procedure. The upgrade process automatically corrects any functionality from Drupal 6 that was removed in Drupal 7 and updates content to use new features where possible.

Before beginning the upgrade process, it is imperative that you make a backup of your site and test the upgrade procedure on a test instance of your site before upgrading your production site. Contributed modules may require additional steps to upgrade them from Drupal 6 to Drupal 7. We covered some of these cases in the last chapter as we reviewed some of the new contributed modules that are available for Drupal 7. If we did not cover a module you are using in Drupal 6, refer to the project page for that module on Drupal.org to see if any additional steps need to be taken during the upgrade process.

You should also review any contributed modules you are using to make sure they have a Drupal 7 version available or that there is a suitable alternative which provides similar functionality if there isn't an upgrade.

To demonstrate the upgrade process, a simple Drupal 6 site has been created and the Devel module (http://drupal.org/project/devel) has been used to populate the site with sample data. The site includes a blog, forums, a bunch of comments, and regular pages and stories. The home page looks like the following screenshot:

To upgrade your site, you will have to perform the following steps. These steps need to be done in one sitting so that your login information is not lost and the process is not interrupted:

1. Back up your site's database. If you are using MySQL, you can use phpMyAdmin to export your database to a file. You can also use the `Backup and Migrate` module (`http://drupal.org/project/backup_migrate`) to make a backup of your database. The `Backup and Migrate` module has the added benefit of being smart enough to know which tables you don't need to back up (for example, cache tables), and it can back up any data source.

2. Back up your entire Drupal 6 installation. Pay careful attention to make sure that you have all of the information in your `sites` directory since this is where configuration files, contributed modules, custom code, and custom themes are stored. You should also back up any files that may have been uploaded to the server as well as any other custom code you may have on the site. You may even want to make two backups—one of the entire site, and one of just your `sites` directory, additional files, and other customized code. Log in to your site as the first user. This user will be needed to run the upgrade process.

3. Set your site to be offline. This prevents users from accessing the system and interfering with the upgrade process or from seeing the site when it is not fully operational. To put your site into offline mode, you will need to visit the site maintenance page of your Drupal 6 site. This can be reached at `http://www.yoursite.com/admin/settings/site-maintenance` or by clicking on **Administer | Site configuration | Site maintenance** from the menu:

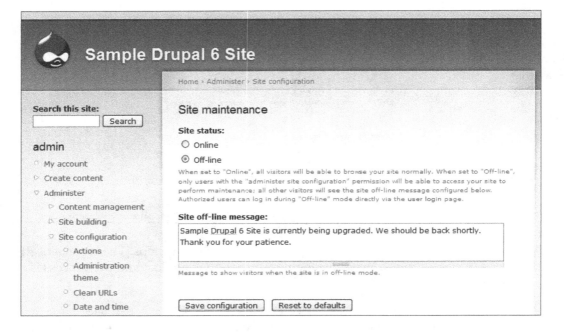

4. After your site is in maintenance mode, you will need to disable any custom modules and custom themes that you installed. This will ensure they do not interfere with the upgrade process. As part of this, you will need to disable your site theme and return to a core theme such as Garland or Bluemarine. If you have deactivated these themes, you will need to reactivate one or the other.

5. Remove all of the old Drupal files from your site including any old Drupal 6 modules and themes. This will prevent the old files from conflicting with Drupal 7.

6. Download and unpack Drupal 7 if you have not done so already and copy it to the root directory for your site.

7. Copy the information from your old `sites` directory back to your site. Especially make sure to copy your `settings.php` file as well as any files that were uploaded to the site. You do not need to copy any Drupal 6 themes or modules back to your site.

8. If you customized core files such as `.htaccess` or `robots.txt`, you should reapply the changes rather than copying the files over. This will preserve changes made from Drupal 6 to Drupal 7.

9. Double check your `settings.php` file to make sure that it has all of the correct information for your site.

10. Run `update.php` by visiting `http://www.yoursite.com/update.php`. This will start the upgrade process.

11. Drupal will first display a message describing the upgrade process and reminding you to back up your database and source code, as shown in the following screenshot:

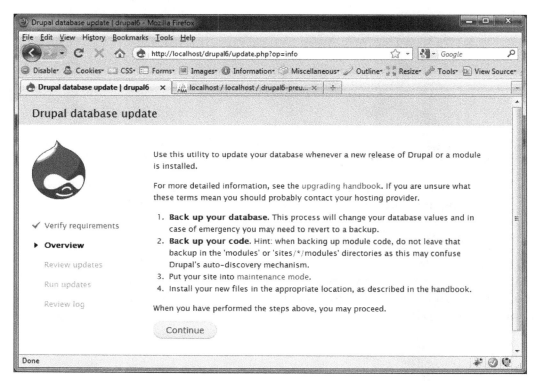

12. After you click on the **Continue** button, Drupal will display a screen describing the updates that will be applied during the upgrade process.

13. Selecting the **Apply pending updates** button will begin the upgrade process. During this procedure, you should not interrupt the installation process or refresh the page. The page will automatically update to show you the progress of the upgrade as each update is applied.

When the upgrade is complete, Drupal will display a log describing the changes that were made as well as any errors that may have occurred. After you complete the upgrade, you can continue to either the front page of your site or the administration section.

Creating custom installation profiles

Installation profiles allow you to easily install Drupal with additional functionality included by default. For example, you can set up an installation profile to:

- Automatically add additional users to your site
- Add additional roles to your site
- Set up permissions for default users
- Add additional contributed modules to your site
- Add additional themes to your site
- Add default content to your site
- Modify common settings to speed setup

As you can see, the options for installation profiles are nearly limitless in Drupal 7. This is especially true because installation profiles are essentially modules now, and you can do nearly anything you want to with a custom module in an installation profile.

If you are only maintaining a single site, you probably won't want to create an installation profile, but if you are setting up many new customer sites each month, you should definitely consider building a custom installation profile to set up a base site that you can then extend to meet each customer's specific needs.

Components of an installation profile

Let's start by looking at the files that make up an installation profile.

- The .info file: The .info file names and describes the installation profile and gives compatibility information so the installer can verify that the correct minimum requirements for the profile have been met and set up the correct modules.
- The .profile file: The .profile file allows you to modify the site configuration form so you can request additional information from the user performing the installation or set default values for the installation. This file is specified within the .info file.
- The .install file: The .install file contains the code that should be run to set up the new site after the core Drupal installation has completed.

The .info file

Let's look at the contents of the `.info` file. In this example, we will look at the default profile that ships with Drupal. Let's look at the entire file and then break down each section independently.

```
; $Id: default.info,v 1.8 2009/11/10 17:27:54 webchick Exp $
name = Drupal
description = Create a Drupal site with the most commonly used
    features pre-installed.
version = VERSION
core = 7.x
dependencies[] = block
dependencies[] = color
dependencies[] = comment
dependencies[] = dashboard
dependencies[] = help
dependencies[] = image
dependencies[] = menu
dependencies[] = path
dependencies[] = taxonomy
dependencies[] = dblog
dependencies[] = search
dependencies[] = shortcut
dependencies[] = toolbar
dependencies[] = field_ui
dependencies[] = file
dependencies[] = rdf
files[] = default.profile

; Information added by drupal.org packaging script on 2009-11-21
version = "7.x-dev"
core = "7.x"
project = "drupal"
datestamp = "1258805146"
```

As you can see, the file uses a basic INI style format that provides information in a series of name-value pairs using the format:

```
name = value
```

Names that end with square brackets [] are treated as arrays when they are read. Any lines which start with a semi-colon are treated as comments and ignored when the file is read.

The first line in the file is used by the version control system to insert version information. If you create your own installation profile, you should replace this line with:

```
; $Id;
```

The next four lines identify the name of the profile, a description of the profile, the current version of the profile, and the version of core this profile is compatible with.

```
name = Drupal
description = Create a Drupal site with the most commonly used
    features pre-installed.
version = VERSION
core = 7.x
```

You should modify at least the name and description values for your installation profile if you are building a custom installation profile.

> The default installation profile sets the version variable based on the value generated by the packaging script. If you are not posting your profile to Drupal.org to share with other site administrators, you will need to maintain this value yourself.

The dependencies lines list all of the modules that must be enabled for the profile to install correctly. The Drupal installer will automatically enable these modules for you.

```
dependencies[]  = block
dependencies[]  = color
dependencies[]  = comment
dependencies[]  = dashboard
. . .
```

You can add or remove any additional modules that you will need to use your installation profile. If you are using a third-party module, make sure that it has been deployed to your site before the installation profile has been run.

The `files` variable defines any files that are needed to run the installation profile. Typically, this will just be your `.profile` file. However, you may also include additional files if the setup you do is very complex. To include additional files, simply add another `files[]` line with the name of the file you want to include, as shown below:

```
files[] = default.profile
```

The remainder of the file contains information included automatically by the Drupal packaging script. You do not need to add these to your file if you are building a custom installation profile.

The .profile file

The `.profile` file allows you to alter the installation and change which forms are presented to the user.

The following hooks can be added to your `.profile` file:

- `hook_profile_details`: This hook allows you to define a language that will be used during the installation. If a language is set here, the user will be unable to set the language during the installation. In Drupal 6, you would also define the name and description for the profile. You don't need to do that anymore since the name and description are provided in the `.info` file. For more information on this hook see:

  `http://api.drupal.org/api/function/example_profile_details/7`.

- `hook_install_tasks`: This hook allows you to define additional tasks that will be performed at the end of the installation process. Each task will be executed in the order they are defined. A task can be one of three types:

  - **normal**: The function will be run and can return either HTML to be displayed to the user or nothing if processing should continue without further user interaction.
  - **form**: The function will return a form definition using the standard Form API. The installer will present the form to the user and then submit the form to the function you define for processing.
  - **batch**: The function will return a batch definition, which will be run by the installer. For more information about batches, see:

  `http://api.drupal.org/api/function/batch_set/7`.

  For complete documentation on this hook see:

  `http://api.drupal.org/api/function/hook_install_tasks/7`.

- `hook_install_tasks_alter`: This hook allows you to change, replace, or remove tasks that are to be run by the installation process. You can modify any of the tasks that will be run from the time the installation profile is selected until the installation completes. This is especially useful if you want to override functionality provided by the core installer. For more information on this hook, see:

  `http://api.drupal.org/api/function/hook_install_tasks_alter/7`.

- `hook_form_alter`: This hook allows you to modify a form before it is displayed. This allows you to add or remove elements from the form or modify existing elements within the form. `hook_form_alter` is widely used within Drupal to make modifications to forms. For complete documentation, visit:

  `http://api.drupal.org/api/function/hook_form_alter/7.`

As with any Drupal hook, you will need to replace the word "hook" with the name of your profile so Drupal can correctly find the function. Therefore, if your profile is named `drupal_rocks`, your function that implements `hook_profile_details` should be named `drupal_rocks_profile_details`.

The .install file

The `.install` file is where you will perform most of your configuration and setup work after the installation has completed.

You only need to implement one function in this file, `hook_install`. If you have created custom modules, this is the same function that runs when the module is installed. Complete instructions for `hook_install` are available at:

`http://api.drupal.org/api/function/hook_install/7.`

Let's look at the `standard.install` file provided with Drupal to get an idea of what is possible. Rather than looking at the entire file at once, let's break it into sections. If you want to see the entire file, it is located in the `profiles/standard` directory of your Drupal installation.

File structure

The basic structure of the file looks like the following:

```php
<?php
// $Id: default.install,v 1.18 2009/11/10 17:27:54 webchick Exp $

/**
 * Implement hook_install().
 *
 * Perform actions to set up the site for this profile.
 */
function default_install() {
  //Actual work happens here!
  ...
}
```

The file starts out with the opening PHP tag `<?php`. Then, the `Id` is again entered automatically by the version control system. If you are developing your own installation module, you should simply enter `// $Id$`. Do not enter all the remaining information; that will be generated automatically. Next, the file has a comment (the information starting with `/**` and ending with `*/`) stating what the function does. This is good coding practice and helps other people to understand what you are trying to do. It can also help you understand your own code if it's been a little while since you wrote it. You may even want to include a summary of what the installation will do, and why, to remind yourself after you have been away from the code for a while.

After the comment comes the actual implementation of `hook_install`. Since this profile is named default, the function is called `default_install`. The logic of the function is then included and the function ends with a closing curly bracket. By convention, Drupal files do not include the optional closing PHP tag after all functions have been written, so the file ends there.

Block creation

Now, let's look at the actual logic being performed within the profile. The first section of code begins by defining several blocks which are then added to the default display.

```
// Enable some standard blocks.
  $values = array(
    array(
      'module' => 'system',
      'delta' => 'main',
      'theme' => 'garland',
      'status' => 1,
      'weight' => 0,
      'region' => 'content',
      'pages' => '',
      'cache' => -1,
    ),
    ...
    array(
      'module' => 'user',
      'delta' => 'new',
      'theme' => 'seven',
      'status' => 1,
      'weight' => 0,
      'region' => 'dashboard_sidebar',
      'pages' => '',
      'cache' => -1,
```

```
    ),
  );
  $query = db_insert('block')->fields(array('module', 'delta',
    'theme', 'status', 'weight', 'region', 'pages', 'cache'));
  foreach ($values as $record) {
    $query->values($record);
  }
  $query->execute();
```

Each block is loaded into the $values array. Each module defines the name of the module, which defines the block as well as the delta or unique ID of the block within the module. The theme setting controls which theme the block should be active for and the status variable controls if the block is enabled (1) or disabled (2). The region variable controls where the block should be displayed within the page and weight controls the position within the region. The pages setting controls which pages the block should be shown on. In the case of the default installation profile, they are shown on all pages. If you want to only show the block on some pages, you should also include the visibility parameter. The cache setting controls whether or not the block can be cached to optimize performance. By default, all blocks are set to -1, which means do not cache. You can change this to a variety of values for fine-grained caching control. For a complete list of fields that can be set for a block and their possible values, see:

http://api.drupal.org/api/function/block_schema/7.

The next several lines set up a query to insert the blocks into the database using the new DBTNG layer and then execute the query to save all of the new blocks. We will review the DBTNG layer more in Chapter 6, so don't worry about the actual syntax too much for now.

Node type definition

The next section adds some default node types that editors can use to add content to the site.

```
// Insert default user-defined node types into the database. For a
  complete
// list of available node type attributes, refer to the node type
  API
// documentation at:
  http://api.drupal.org/api/HEAD/function/hook_node_info.
$types = array(
  array(
    'type' => 'page',
    'name' => st('Page'),
    'base' => 'node_content',
```

```
      'description' => st("Use <em>pages</em> for your static
        content, such as an 'About us' page."),
      'custom' => 1,
      'modified' => 1,
      'locked' => 0,
    ),
    array(
      'type' => 'article',
      'name' => st('Article'),
      'base' => 'node_content',
      'description' => st('Use <em>articles</em> for time-specific
        content like news, press releases or blog posts.'),
      'custom' => 1,
      'modified' => 1,
      'locked' => 0,
    ),
  );

  foreach ($types as $type) {
    $type = node_type_set_defaults($type);
    node_type_save($type);
  }
```

In this case, two node types are being added—a `page` node type and an `article` node type. The installation profile defines the `type`, `name`, and `description` for each node type. These are all fairly straightforward. However, note that the `st()` function is called to provide translations rather than `t()`. This is done because the `install` function is called during the install process and the full localization system may not be available yet. The profile also sets the base for the `node` type, which tells Drupal which module will control the functionality of the node. By setting `custom` to 1, the installation profile instructs Drupal that this node type should be treated as if it were created by a user and that it is not defined by a module. Setting `locked` to 0 indicates that the name of the content type can be modified by an administrator.

After basic information has been defined for each node type, the installation profile begins to save each type individually. Before saving the type, it calls `node_type_set_defaults`, which builds a type object and adds additional default information to it. The new node type is then saved with a call to `node_type_save`.

Additional default settings

The installation profile then uses the same technique of defining an array of information and then saving it to build RDF-mapping information for each type as well as taxonomies and fields. Because these substantially use the same techniques as creating blocks and node types, we will omit a line by line discussion of these.

Between setting up the RDF mappings and creating taxonomies, the installation profile sets the values of some variables in the database using the following lines:

```
// Default page to not be promoted and have comments disabled.
variable_set('node_options_page', array('status'));
variable_set('comment_page', COMMENT_NODE_HIDDEN);

// Don't display date and author information for page nodes by
   default.
variable_set('node_submitted_page', FALSE);

// Enable user picture support and set the default to a square
   thumbnail option.
variable_set('user_pictures', '1');
variable_set('user_picture_dimensions', '1024x1024');
variable_set('user_picture_file_size', '800');
variable_set('user_picture_style', 'thumbnail');
```

All of these lines use the `variable_set` function to change the value of the variables. You can get a list of all variables defined within Drupal using the Devel module (`http://drupal.org/project/devel`).

Setting up permissions and roles

Skipping down to the end of the file after all of the fields have been created, the installation profile sets some default permissions for the Anonymous and Authenticated roles using a call to `user_role_grant_permissions`.

```
// Enable default permissions for system roles.
user_role_grant_permissions(DRUPAL_ANONYMOUS_RID, array('access
   content', 'use text format 1'));
user_role_grant_permissions(DRUPAL_AUTHENTICATED_RID, array('access
   content', 'access comments', 'post comments', 'post comments
   without approval', 'use text format 1'));
```

If you are creating your own installation profile, which activates additional modules, you may want to activate additional permissions for these users.

The installation profile also creates a new role for the administrator and sets some default permissions:

```
// Create a default role for site administrators, with all available
permissions assigned.
$admin_role = new stdClass();
$admin_role->name = 'administrator';
user_role_save($admin_role);
user_role_grant_permissions($admin_role->rid,
  array_keys(module_invoke_all('permission')));
```

The new role is set up by creating an object to store the role and then saving it with a call to `user_role_save`. The permissions are granted by first calling `module_invoke_all('permission')`. This loads all available permissions for all modules which have been enabled, thus giving the administrator role all available permissions.

To ensure that the administrator role stays up to date, the installation profile assigns the administrator role as the system admin role by updating the appropriate system variable.

```
// Set this as the administrator role.
variable_set('user_admin_role', $admin_role->rid);
```

Next the profile rebuilds the menu system to ensure the cache is fresh and that all modules which were installed are correctly updated:

```
// Update the menu router information.
menu_rebuild();
```

Theme configuration

Finally, the installation profile activates the Seven theme and sets it up for use as the administration theme.

```
// Enable the admin theme.
db_update('system')
  ->fields(array('status' => 1))
  ->condition('type', 'theme')
  ->condition('name', 'seven')
  ->execute();
variable_set('admin_theme', 'seven');
variable_set('node_admin_theme', '1');
```

To do this, it again executes a query using the new DBTNG syntax and then sets a couple of variables to finalize the installation. Don't worry about the syntax of the update query too much right now; we will definitely explore this in more detail in Chapter 7.

After the Seven theme has been installed, the installation profile ends and the installation continues. Remember, because the Drupal core has been installed and all of your modules have been activated, when the `install` function runs, there is a wide range of actions you can perform during this routine.

Summary

In this chapter, we took a step back and looked at the changes to the installation process. We also looked at the process for upgrading your Drupal 6 sites to Drupal 7, so you can utilize all of the great new features of Drupal 7.

We also covered setting up custom installation profiles, so you can install multiple sites using the same basic configuration.

In the next chapter, we will look at a variety of changes made to the theming system to make extending themes and developing your own themes easier.

Site Building with Drupal 7

One of Drupal's strengths has always been the ease with which you can add, edit, and organize the information on your site. There are several key changes to Drupal 7 that will make your life as a content editor easier, including:

- Improved interface for adding content makes your work more productive.
- The ability to add and modify fields in Core rather than using the contributed CCK module makes it easier to customize and validate the information on your site. This functionality was built from and replaces the contributed CCK module.
- Improved categorization with taxonomies.
- Built-in support for image handling.
- Improved support for handling files and attaching files to content.
- More control over text formats.

In this chapter, we will cover all of these new features and enhancements. By the end of the chapter, you should be able to create custom content types with custom fields, add content to your site, translate your content, and leverage all of the new Drupal 7 functionality.

Creating content

Creating content for your site is at the core of any Content Management System like Drupal. The primary changes for Drupal 7 relate to an updated interface. Let's look at the new interface in detail.

Selecting a content type to create

To create content in Drupal 7, first log in to your site and then click on **Content** from the site toolbar. Drupal will now display the new Content Administration page.

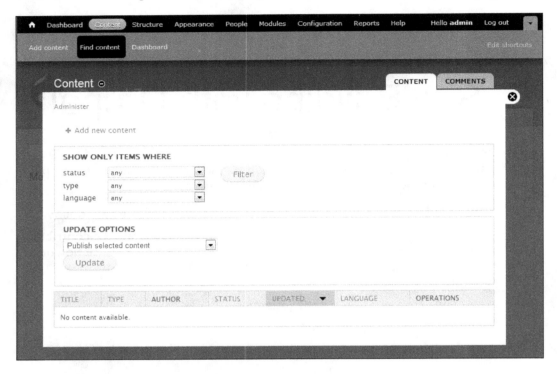

In Drupal 6, this page could be displayed by selecting **Administer | Content Management | Content** from the Navigation menu.

From here, click on the **Add new content** link. Drupal will now display a page allowing you to select the type of content you want to create. Depending on the modules you have installed and enabled, you will have different content types available.

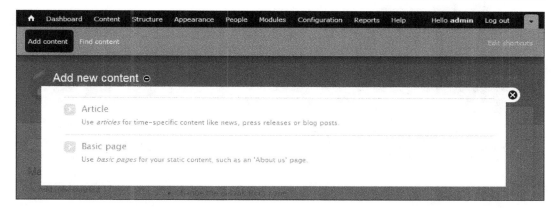

In previous versions of Drupal, this page could be reached by selecting the **Create Content** link from the Navigation menu.

You can also select the type of content to add using the shortcut bar. You can access the shortcut bar by clicking on the toggle at the far right of the toolbar:

The shortcut bar has a list of links in it that can be used to quickly access commonly-used functionality, and it appears as follows:

You can customize the links in the shortcut bar and users can use either the default set of shortcuts or they can have their own. We will look into building shortcuts in the next chapter.

Now select the type of content you want to create. For this example, we will use the **Basic page** type.

Content UI

The interface to create content has been altered drastically from Drupal 6. Let's go through the interface in detail.

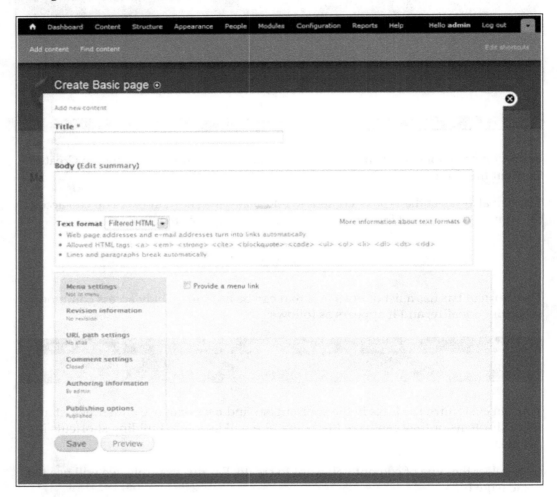

The top section of the page should be familiar to experienced editors. This is the place to enter your title as well as the full text of the page. In a departure from previous versions, the node summary, which is used when multiple nodes are displayed on a page, is an entirely separate optional field.

Creating node summaries

To create a node summary, click on the **Edit summary** link next to the **Full text** label. Drupal will display a second field that can be used to define your summary.

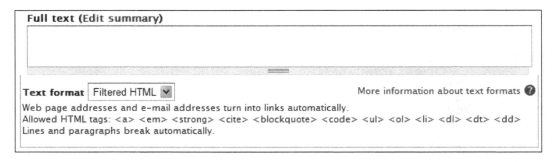

The **Summary** entry in Drupal 7 is much easier for new content editors to work with. There is now a separate text area where the Summary can be entered. Of course, you can still use a subset of the full text by simply leaving the **Summary** blank.

Formatting text

Below the **Full text** field, you will find a list of available text formats that can be applied to the text field.

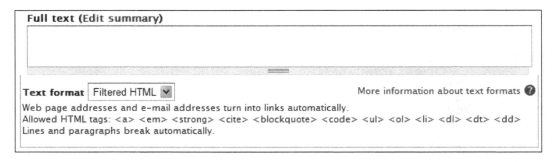

This display is much more compact than that in previous versions making it much easier to select a text format to apply. Text formats are used to limit which HTML tags can be inserted into the full text field. By default, Drupal 7 includes **Plain Text**, **Filtered HTML**, and **Full HTML** formats. If you enable the PHP filter module, you will also have access to the **PHP code** text format. These are all configured identically to the Drupal 6 Input Filters of the same name.

Text formats can be edited by selecting **Configuration** from the administration toolbar and then selecting **Text formats** from the **Content Authoring** section. The interface for creating text formats is very similar to the Drupal 6 interface for creating and editing input formats. You can still assign text formats to roles and control which filters run on the input. However, some of the filters have been renamed and additional information has been added to the display to help you select which filters you want to apply. The filters map as follows:

- **Convert URLs into links** was called URL filter in Drupal 6
- The **Convert line breaks** filter was called Line break converter in Drupal 6
- **Correct broken HTML** was called HTML corrector in Drupal 6
- **Escape all HTML** was part of the Drupal 6 HTML filter that was broken up to improve usability
- **Limit allowed HTML tags** was also part of the Drupal 6 HTML filter
- The **PHP evaluator** remains as is from Drupal 6

Additional node properties

Below the text format, you will find a set of vertical tabs containing all of the optional properties you can apply to your new node:

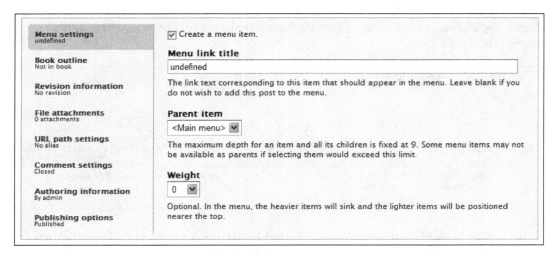

This display replaces the collapsible field sets used in Drupal 6. The new display is much better looking and easier to use. The contents of each tab are similar to prior versions.

Creating new content types with custom fields

Drupal 6 provided the ability to add new content types, which represented different types of content on your site. Visitors could then search the different types of content and you could change how they were displayed. However, Drupal 6 by itself was pretty limited as to the types of information you could attach to new content types. To get around these limitations, a majority of sites installed the contributed CCK module (short for Content Construction Kit). This module allowed administrators to add fields to a content type. Each field could be configured with the type of information it could contain, how it was validated, and what type of input control was used in edit forms. Because creating new content types was done so often and because a majority of sites used CCK, the Drupal core team decided to add much of the functionality from CCK into Drupal core.

Creating a custom content type

Content types are created within the **Structure** portion of the Administration interface. Start by clicking on the **Structure** link in the toolbar and then click on **Content types** from the **Structure** page. Depending on what modules you have enabled, the resulting page will appear similar to the following screenshot:

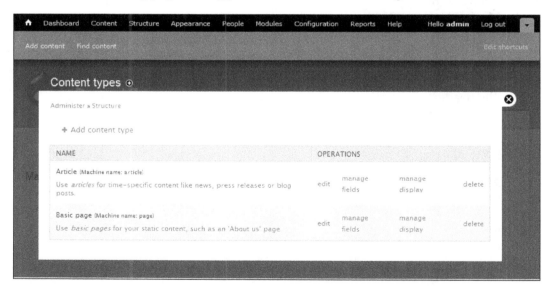

To add a new content type, click on the **Add content type** link just under the header. Drupal will now display a form that allows you to enter information about the content type you want to create. Let's look at each section of the form.

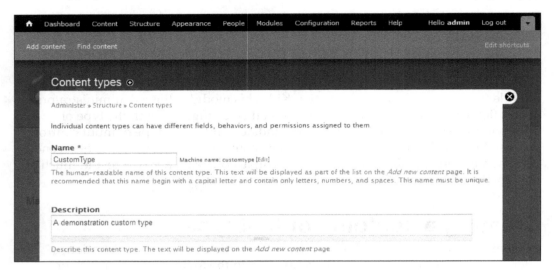

The top portion of the section allows you to name your content type and set a **Description** for the type. A nice new feature of Drupal 7 is the automatic generation of the **Machine name**. Of course, you can also enter your own machine name by clicking on the **Edit** link next to the default machine name.

Additional content type properties

Below the header information is another set of vertical tabs, which allow you to configure additional properties for the content type.

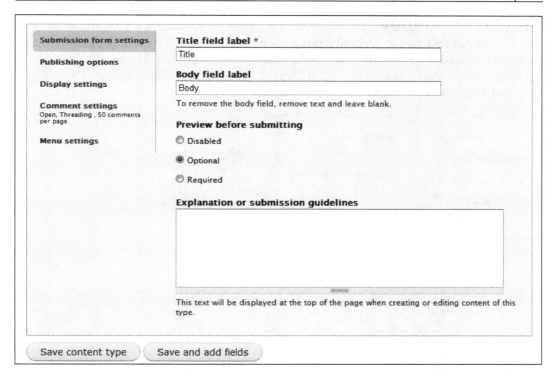

The **Submission form settings** and **Publishing options** are very similar to Drupal 6 and are mostly self explanatory, so we'll leave them for now.

Display settings

The **Display settings** section is new to Drupal 7 and appears as follows:

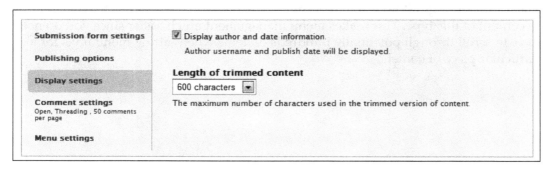

The display settings are used to control whether or not the author of each post is identified in the display as well as the total length of the teaser or trimmed post when the node is displayed in a listing with other nodes.

Comment settings

The **Comment settings** in Drupal 7 have been greatly refined from Drupal 6. Drupal 6 offered nine different sections of configuration and over 20 different choices taking up two screens worth of real estate. In Drupal 7, the list has been reduced to four basic settings and only eight different controls.

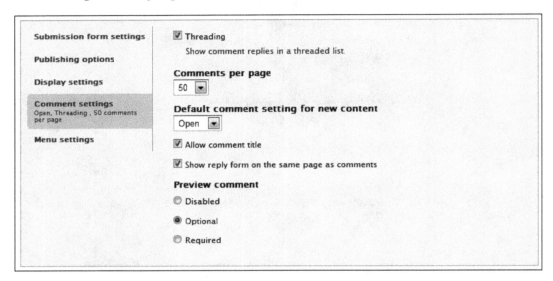

The remaining controls serve the same function that they did in Drupal 6. The controls which were removed were not widely used and reasonable defaults have been inserted instead.

Menu settings

The **Menu settings** allow you to determine which menus are allowed to contain links to content of this type. This makes menu management much easier since you do not have to scroll through potentially hundreds of items when setting menu links for a particular piece of content.

Submission form settings

Publishing options

Display settings

Comment settings
Open, Threading , 50 comments
per page

Menu settings

Available menus

☑ Main menu

☐ Management

☐ Navigation

☐ Secondary menu

☐ User menu

The menus available to place links in for this content type

Default parent item

<Main menu> ▼

Choose the menu item to be the default parent for a new link in the content authoring
form.

You can select as many menus as you would like and set a default menu for the
content type. This can save you and your content editors a great deal of time while
building content.

After you are happy with your content type, simply click on **Save content type** to
save the new content type in the system. If you plan to add fields immediately, you
can also click on **Save and add fields**.

Field API

Now that we have looked at the modifications to creating content types in Drupal
7, let's look at the new Field API that allows us to define custom fields for our new
content type. There are a variety of ways to access the fields for a content type. From
the list of content types, you can click on **manage fields**, or if you are already editing
a content type, you can click on the **MANAGE FIELDS** tab.

After you select the **MANAGE FIELDS** tab, you will be taken to a list of the existing
fields for your content type, with a quick way to add either a new or existing field.

The **Title** and **Body** fields are now fields. You are required to keep the **Title** field, but you may modify or even remove the **Body** field. This gives a great deal of additional flexibility to your content types.

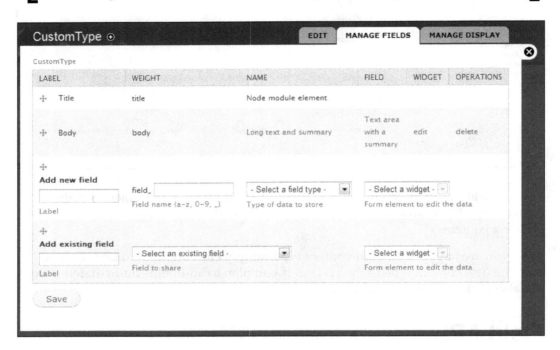

To create a new field, simply enter the label you want to use for the field as well as the name of the field. The name is used to identify the field internally and must consist of only lowercase letters, numbers, and underscores. After naming the field, you will need to select the field type. The available field types in Drupal 7 are:

- Boolean
- Decimal
- File
- Float
- Image
- Integer
- List
- List (numeric)

- List (text)
- Long text
- Long text and summary
- Term reference
- Text

Many of these field types will be familiar to past users of CCK. However, there are also some important new field types that were either not present in prior versions or required extensions to CCK. These include **File**, **Image**, **Long text and summary**, and **Term reference**.

After you select the type of field, you will need to select the widget to use when displaying the field. In Drupal 7, these include:

Widget name	Applicable field types
Select List	Boolean, List, List (numeric), List (text), Term reference
Checkboxes/ radio buttons	Boolean, List, List (numeric), List (text), Term reference
Single on/off checkbox	Boolean
Text field	Decimal, Float, Integer, Text
File	File
Image	Image
Text area (multiple rows)	Long text
Text area with a summary	Long text and summary
Autocomplete term widget (tagging)	Term reference

Let's look in more detail at each field type.

Boolean fields

Boolean fields allow you to add fields that only have two possible values. Typically, these are yes/no, true/false, on/off, and so on. Let's add a sample field. For the field label, enter **Is Drupal the best CMS**, for the field name enter **is_drupal_best**, select **Boolean** for the field type, and **Check boxes/radio buttons** for the Widget. Click on **Save** to add the new field.

After the field is saved, Drupal will present a form where you can set the options for the field. The contents of this form will vary depending on the type of widget you select, but for our configuration it will appear as follows:

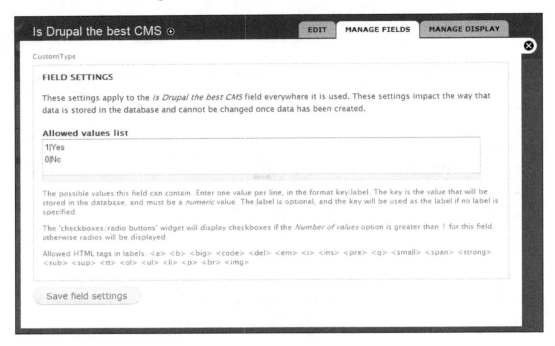

Let's look more at **Allowed values list**. The **Allowed values list** field allows you to specify the options you want to display, with the value for each option. Typically, a Boolean field will use 0 for the option representing no/false/off and either 1 or -1 for the option representing yes/true/on.

 The options will display when the field is being edited in the same order as the values in **Allowed values list**. It's a good idea to put the most common value first.

After setting the allowed values, click on **Save field settings**. Drupal will now prompt you for information related to default values, whether or not the field is required, and help text as shown below:

Updated field *Is Drupal the best CMS* field settings.

CUSTOMTYPE SETTINGS

These settings apply only to the *Is Drupal the best CMS* field when used in the *CustomType* type.

Label *

Is Drupal the best CMS

☐ Required field

Help text

Instructions to present to the user below this field on the editing form.
Allowed HTML tags: <a> <b> <big> <code> <del> <em> <i> <ins> <pre> <q> <small> <span> <strong> <sub> <sup> <tt> <ol> <ul> <li> <p>
 <img>

DEFAULT VALUE
The default value for this field, used when creating new content.

Is Drupal the best CMS

○ N/A

○ Yes

○ No

IS DRUPAL THE BEST CMS FIELD SETTINGS

These settings apply to the *Is Drupal the best CMS* field everywhere it is used.

Number of values

Maximum number of values users can enter for this field.

Allowed values list

1|Yes
0|No

The possible values this field can contain. Enter one value per line, in the format key|label. The key is the value that will be stored in the database, and must be a *numeric* value. The label is optional, and the key will be used as the label if no label is specified.

The 'checkboxes/radio buttons' widget will display checkboxes if the *Number of values* option is greater than 1 for this field, otherwise radios will be displayed.

Allowed HTML tags in labels: <a> <b> <big> <code> <del> <em> <i> <ins> <pre> <q> <small> <span> <strong> <sub> <sup> <tt> <ol> <ul> <li> <p>
 <img>

Save settings

You can also override the default label and change the allowable values. Feel free to modify these settings as needed. For this example, the defaults are fine. When you are finished, click on **Save settings**.

You will now be returned to the list of fields and our new field will be displayed:

	Is Drupal the best CMS	field_is_drupal_best	Boolean	Check boxes/radio buttons	edit	delete

You can modify the widget used to display your field by clicking on the name of the active widget. After modifying the widget, review your options to make sure they are still valid for the new display.

The Boolean field is new to Drupal 7 and did not exist in the base installation of CCK for Drupal 6. In Drupal 6, the Integer type was typically used when a Boolean was needed.

Numeric fields (Decimal, Float, and Integer)

The Decimal, Float, and Integer fields are used to store numeric information. The Decimal and Float fields both allow numbers with decimals to be entered, while the Integer field only allows whole numbers. The Float and Decimal fields store their data in different types within the database, and the Decimal field gives you additional control over the precision and scale of the values which can be input. In all three cases, Drupal takes care of all input validation for you, so you don't have to worry about someone trying to enter "two" as a value. Drupal will also make sure the numbers fall within the range of valid values you specify. Let's take a look at adding a numeric field.

The basic procedure for adding a numeric field is similar to that for adding a Boolean field. First we will set the label and internal name for the field and then select the field type and widget for the field. Both Decimal and Integer types only allow the Text field widget, so our decision will be easy. For this example, we'll label the field **How many years have you used Drupal** and name it **num_years**. The type will be Decimal and the widget Text field.

Make sure to carefully consider what type of field you want to use before adding the field, since you will not be able to change the field type after it has been created.

After you save the basic field information, Drupal will again prompt you for some additional information specific to the Decimal type:

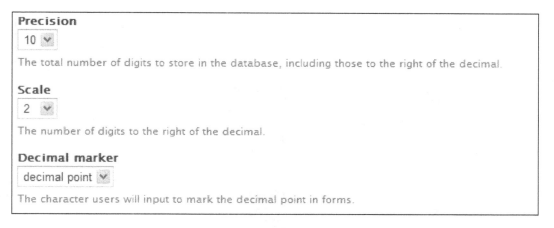

Decimal marker can be set to **decimal point, comma,** or **space** based to match the expectations of your visitors.

 The Integer and Float types do not require you to set any additional settings.

The **Scale** and **Precision** settings work together to determine how the number is stored. If you increase the scale (number of digits to the right of the decimal), you will need to increase the precision as well if you want to retain the same number of overall digits.

After you have set these options to your desired values, click on **Save field settings**. You will now be presented with a set of options that allow you to set minimum and maximum values, as well as the prefix and suffix:

CUSTOM TYPE SETTINGS

These settings apply only to the *How many years have you used Drupal* field when used in the *Custom Type* type.

Label *

> How many years have you used Drupal

The human-readable label for this field.

☐ Required
  Check if a value must be provided.

Minimum

> 0

The minimum value that should be allowed in this field. Leave blank for no minimum.

Help text

>

Instructions to present to the user below this field on the editing form.
Allowed HTML tags: <a> <b> <big> <code> <del> <em> <i> <ins> <pre> <q> <small> <span> <strong> <sub> <sup> <tt> <ol> <ul> <li> <p>
 <img>

Maximum

> 100

The maximum value that should be allowed in this field. Leave blank for no maximum.

Prefix

>

Define a string that should be prefixed to the value, like '$ ' or '€ '. Leave blank for none. Separate singular and plural values with a pipe ('pound|pounds').

Suffix

> years

Define a string that should suffixed to the value, like ' m', ' kb/s'. Leave blank for none. Separate singular and plural values with a pipe ('pound|pounds').

DEFAULT VALUE

The default value for this field, used when creating new content.

How many years have you used Drupal

>

These settings apply to both Decimal and Integer fields. The **Prefix** and **Suffix** fields are valuable tools for giving your site visitors and editors more information about the type of data that is expected. After you have customized the settings, select **Save settings** to finalize the field. You can change these options after the field has been saved by clicking on the **Edit** link in the list of fields.

All three of these field types existed within CCK for Drupal 6 and are very similar to their Drupal 6 counterparts.

File fields

File fields can be used to allow editors to attach files to content. For example, you can attach training manuals or product data sheets to your content. Drupal will handle uploading files to the server, ensuring they have the proper type and are smaller than the maximum size. The basic procedure to add a file field is the same as the other fields we have looked at so far. Specify the label and name for your field and set the type to **File**. The only available widget is **File**. The custom settings for this type are as follows:

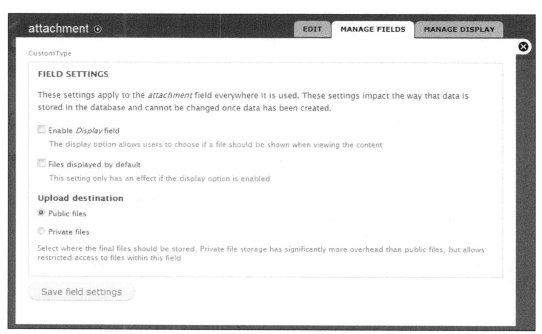

The **Enable Display field** setting is used to determine whether or not the file can be viewed when the node it is attached to is viewed. The **Files displayed by default** setting is used to determine if a link to the file should be included by default. This can be overridden for any file that is attached to the node. **Upload destination** determines if files will be stored within the **Public files** directory, which can be accessed directly by visitors, or if the files will be stored in the **Private files** directory, which is controlled by Drupal allowing you to add additional security for how the files are accessed.

After these basic options are set and saved, you will be taken to another screen where you can edit more advanced options as shown below:

Allowed file extensions

txt

Separate extensions with a space or comma and do not include the leading dot. Leaving this blank will allow users to upload a file with any extension.

File directory

Optional subdirectory within the upload destination where files will be stored. Do not include preceding or trailing slashes.

Maximum upload size

Enter a value like "512" (bytes), "80 KB" (kilobytes) or "50 MB" (megabytes) in order to restrict the allowed file size. If left empty the file sizes will be limited only by PHP's maximum post and file upload sizes (current limit *64 MB*)

▢ Enable *Description* field

The description field allows users to enter a description about the uploaded file.

The **Allowed file extensions** setting allows you to determine which types of files can be added. When files are uploaded, Drupal will validate that they are of the correct type. This is an important setting to help ensure that visitors are not uploading malicious content to your site. The **Maximum upload size** setting is also important to make sure that your server is not swamped with exceptionally large files. The **File directory** setting allows you to segregate files within your upload destination. This can be a great way of grouping files on your site so you always know the source of the file. In Drupal 6, you could achieve similar functionality using the FileField extension for CCK.Image fields

Image fields are an exciting and much sought-after inclusion in Drupal core. As the name implies, image fields allow you to attach images to your content type. Building an image field follows similar steps to other fields. First set the label and name for your field and then set the type and widget to **image**. The basic options allow you to control where the files are stored and allow you to provide a default image that will be used if the editor does not attach an image when they create an instance of the content type. If you do not have a default image, nothing will be shown if there is no attached image:

After saving these basic options, you will be presented with more advanced options giving you control over what types of images can be inserted as well as how large images can be. Image size can be controlled based on both the total size of the file in bytes, kilobytes, or megabytes, as well as based on the maximum and minimum dimensions of the image in pixels. This gives you a lot of control over what images can be attached to the node and helps when you are ready to theme your content, since you will already know how big the images can be.

The Alt and Title attributes can be activated to allow editors to give additional information about the image. The Alt and Title tags are used for tooltips as well as by screen readers, search engines, and browsers when the image cannot be displayed. In most cases, it is a good idea to enable these options. The full list of options is shown below:

CUSTOMTYPE SETTINGS

These settings apply only to the *image* field when used in the *CustomType* type.

Label *

    image

☐ Required field

Help text

Instructions to present to the user below this field on the editing form
Allowed HTML tags: <a> <b> <big> <code> <del> <em> <i> <ins> <pre> <q> <small> <span> <strong> <sub> <sup> <tt> <ol> <ul> <li> <p>
 <img>

Allowed file extensions

    png, gif, jpg, jpeg

Separate extensions with a space or comma and do not include the leading dot. Leaving this blank will allow users to upload a file with any extension.

File directory

Optional subdirectory within the upload destination where files will be stored. Do not include preceding or trailing slashes.

Maximum image resolution

    [   ] x [   ] pixels

The maximum allowed image size expressed as WIDTHxHEIGHT (e.g. 640x480). Leave blank for no restriction. If a larger image is uploaded, it will be resized to reflect the given width and height. Resizing images on upload will cause the loss of EXIF data in the image.

Minimum image resolution

    [   ] x [   ] pixels

The minimum allowed image size expressed as WIDTHxHEIGHT (e.g. 640x480). Leave blank for no restriction. If a smaller image is uploaded, it will be rejected.

Maximum upload size

Enter a value like "512" (bytes), "80 KB" (kilobytes) or "50 MB" (megabytes) in order to restrict the allowed file size. If left empty the file sizes will be limited only by PHP's maximum post and file upload sizes (current limit *64 MB*)

☐ Enable *Alt* field

   The alt attribute may be used by search engines, screen readers, and when the image cannot be loaded.

☐ Enable *Title* field

   The title attribute is used as a tooltip when the mouse hovers over the image.

Preview image style

    thumbnail ▼

The preview image will be shown while editing the content

In Drupal 6, you could achieve similar functionality using the ImageField module, which required both the FileField module and CCK.List fields

List fields allow editors to select from a list of possible values when they create an instance of the content type. List fields are great when you already have a predefined list of options that can be selected from and the list is reasonably short. As always, we begin by setting the label, name, and type for the new field. When you select a type, you can choose between **List (numeric)** and **List (text)**. The difference between these two types is whether the values which the editor selects are stored in the database as numbers or text. Using a numeric list has a couple of advantages:

- Database size is minimized because numbers can be stored more compactly than text

- Translation can be easier because labels can be mapped more easily than text and the values are not dependent on any specific language

However, using a text list can make it easier to understand the values when you are looking at the database tables directly (that is, with phpMyAdmin).

 When you use text lists, try abbreviating each option so it is only a few characters long. This helps to make the options more understandable while still reducing the amount of space needed to store each option in the database.

For our example, we will label the field **Favorite Drupal 7 Features**, name it **favorite_features**, give it a type of **List (numeric)**, and set the widget to **Select list**. After creating the label, you will need to set the allowable values list. With both types of lists, you will set the allowed values using the following format: **key|label**. For numeric lists, the key will be a number, and for text lists the key can be text. Here are the options for our sample field:

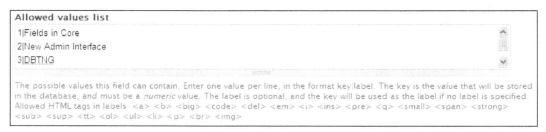

After setting your available values and saving them, you can set a few more options for the field. The first is a **Default value**, which can be used to automatically select a value if the editor creating the node does not select one. The other key setting is the **Number of values** that allows you to set how many selections the user can make from the list. This can be set from 1 to 10 or Unlimited. For example, if you wanted the user to pick their top 3 options, you could set this to 3.

In Drupal 6, you could accomplish this functionality using a CCK text field.

Term Reference fields

Term Reference fields blend taxonomies from Drupal 6 with the field system making it more intuitive for editors, administrators, and themers.

To add a Term Reference field, you will need to create a new taxonomy if you don't have one already. For this example, we will use the **Tags** taxonomy that is installed with Drupal 7. After you have a taxonomy ready, you are ready to create your field. Start by labeling and naming your field. Then, you will need to set the type to **Term Reference** and select a widget. We will use **Autocomplete term widget (tagging)** for now. After you save the new field, you can set the **Vocabulary** to use for the field:

The Term Reference field does not have any new advanced settings that you can apply to it other than setting the default value for the field.

You could achieve similar functionality in Drupal 6 using CCK and the Content Taxonomy module.

Text fields

Text fields are used to add textual information to a content type. Drupal 7 offers several different types of text fields that you can attach to content types including:

- Text
- Long text
- Long text and summary

Each of these types has specific capabilities and uses.

Text field

The text field is designed to store short pieces of text that are one to two lines long or less. The text field allows you to set the maximum length of the field:

> **Maximum length**
>
> 255
>
> The maximum length of the field in characters. Leave blank for an unlimited size.

The text field also allows you to set the size of the textfield, which controls the width of the text box that is used for inputting data. For example, if you set the maximum length of the text to 255 and the size of the textfield to 60, you will be able to see approximately 60 characters in the input box and will be able to add up to 255 characters of text. Drupal takes care of doing all of the validation for you.

> ☐ Required
>
>   Check if a value must be provided.
>
> **Size of textfield** *
>
> 60
>
> **Text processing**
>
> ⦿ Plain text
>
> ◯ Filtered text (user selects input format)

The final option available for the text field is how to process the text. If you select **Plain text**, Drupal will ensure that the text is rendered as plain text and that special HTML characters are properly escaped. If you select **Filtered text**, the user will be able to select a text format from those available to them to apply to the text. Drupal will then automatically apply the text format when the text is rendered.

Long text field

The long text field is designed for use when you need more than a line or two of text. The long text field allows multiple lines of text to be entered and displayed. Much like the simple text field, the long text field allows you to set the maximum length for the text. By default, this is set to unlimited, but you can restrict the length to a shorter value if needed.

The long text field allows you to customize the number of **Rows** that are displayed in the text area when the long text is being edited as well as how text is processed.

You can set the number of rows to be displayed based on the expected length of the text to be entered. If the text will normally be longer, you may want to increase the number of rows displayed.

Long text and summary field

The long text and summary field allows you to add a long text field that also allows the user to enter a short summary for the field, similar to the way body fields work for standard nodes. The basic settings are identical to the long text field, and the advanced settings are similar as well.

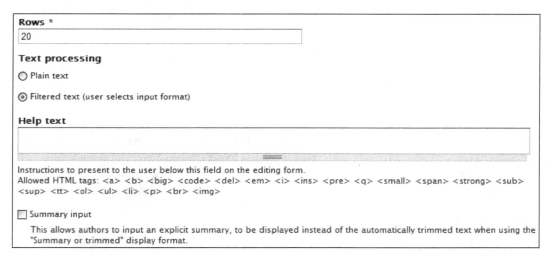

The main differences between the long text and long text and summary fields are the number of rows is set to **20** rather than **5** by default. Also, text processing is set to **Filtered text** rather than **Plain text**, and there is a new **Summary input** setting. The **Summary input** setting determines whether or not authors can override the default trimmed text for the summary.

In Drupal 6, you could create text fields and long text fields using the Text CCK type. The long text and summary field is new to Drupal 7.

Field display

After you have built your content type, you will most likely want to modify the display of the fields. Luckily, Drupal 7 offers a great deal of control over how individual fields are displayed when the content type is displayed in various situations. You can modify the field display by editing your content type and then selecting the **MANAGE DISPLAY** tab. You can also access this page directly from the list of content types.

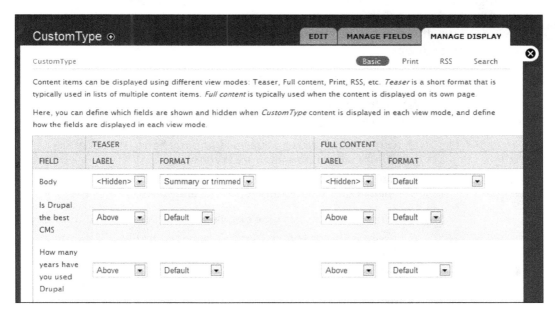

Drupal allows you to set the display format for four main display types: **Basic**, **Print**, **RSS**, and **Search**. Display types may be added or removed depending on what modules you have enabled. Each display type will have one or more sub views that can be configured. For example, the **Basic** display format allows you to configure the **Teaser** view and **FULL CONTENT** view, whereas the **Print** display format only allows the **Print** view to be configured.

 The **Print** display type is added when you enable the Book module.

In all cases, the configuration is similar. You are allowed to modify both the display of the label and the format of the value. The available settings for formatting the label are:

- **<Hidden>**: It causes the label to not be displayed
- **Above**: It causes the label to be displayed over the value
- **Inline**: It causes the label to be displayed to the left of the value

By default, the label is always displayed as bold text with a colon after it. This can be modified by your theme using CSS.

The available formats depend on the field type. Every field also allows **<Hidden>** as a valid value which, as the name implies, removes the field from the display. The following listing shows the available formats by field type with a brief description of what each format does:

Field type	Format
Boolean, List (text), List (numeric)	Default: It displays the value of the field (information to the right of the | symbol when defining allowable values).
	Key: It displays the key of the field (information to the left of the | symbol when defining allowable values).
Integer, Decimal, Float	Default: It displays the number formatted according to the rules defined in the field, including prefixes and suffixes.
	Unformatted: It displays the raw value of the field without formatting.
File	Generic file: It displays an icon and name for the file with a link, so the visitor can download the file.
	Table of files: It displays an icon for the file next to the name of the file which includes a link to download the full file. The size of the file is also included.
	All files are organized into a table.

Attachment	Size
1st Chapter of Drupal 7 First Look	306.67 KB

Field type	Format
	URL to file: The full URL to the file is displayed, but the file is not linked.
Term reference	Link: It displays each selected taxonomy term with a link to browse all nodes that use the term.
	Plain text: It displays the selected taxonomy term with no links to browsing-related nodes.

Field type	Format
Text, Long text	Default: It displays the text formatted according to the field settings and selected text format.
	Plain Text: It displays the text without any formatting applied. HTML tags will be removed.
	Trimmed: It displays a shortened version of the formatted text if it is longer than a certain length.
Long text and summary	The long text and summary uses the same options as the text and long text types, plus it adds a Summary or Trimmed format, which displays the summary if it exists. If no summary has been entered, a trimmed version of the full text of the field will be displayed.

If this level of formatting is insufficient for your needs, you can always build your own template and create a custom theme for your content type. We will explore this more in *Chapter 5, Drupal 7 for Themers*.

Taxonomy changes

Taxonomies in Drupal 7 build on taxonomies in previous versions. However, taxonomies have been promoted to first class objects and can be extended with fields. You can now access the taxonomy system by selecting **Structure** from the administration toolbar. You can then select the **Taxonomy** link.

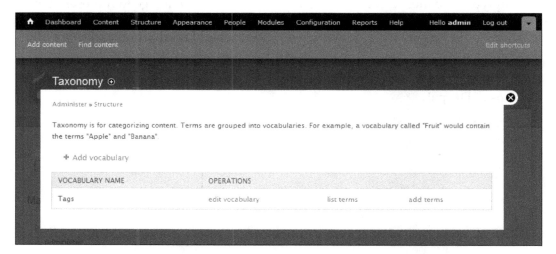

To add a new vocabulary, simply click on the **Add vocabulary** link and add a **Name** and **Description** for the new vocabulary. As you name the vocabulary, Drupal will automatically create the default **Machine name** for you. If you don't like the default machine name, you can always override it. If you edit the vocabulary, you will be taken to a form where you can modify the **Name** and **Description** of the vocabulary.

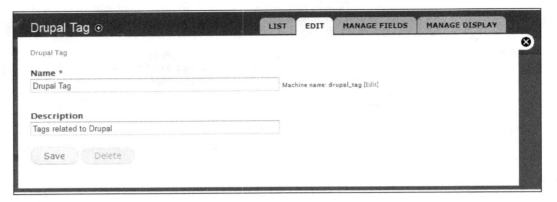

From this screen, you can also access the terms and fields that have been defined for the vocabulary. Terms are accessed via the **LIST** tab, and fields are accessed via the **MANAGE FIELDS** and **MANAGE DISPLAY** tabs.

Fields can be added in exactly the same manner that we used to add fields to custom content type. The most common custom field to create is an image to represent the taxonomy. However, you could also create additional fields to give more information to editors or to help themers or module developers build more complex themes and modules.

When you create a new term, you can set the **Name** and **Description** as in previous versions of Drupal.

Drupal Tag

Name *

Fields in core

Description

Items related to fields in core which was introduced in Drupal 7.

Text format Filtered HTML ▼   More information about text formats 🔵
- Web page addresses and e-mail addresses turn into links automatically.
- Allowed HTML tags: <a> <em> <strong> <cite> <blockquote> <code> <ul> <ol> <li> <dl> <dt> <dd>
- Lines and paragraphs break automatically.

▼ RELATIONS

Parent terms

<root> ▲
▼

Weight *

0

Terms are displayed in ascending order by weight.

(Save)

URL alias

drupal7/fields_in_core

Optionally specify an alternative URL by which this term can be accessed. Use a relative path and don't add a trailing slash or the URL alias won't work.

You can also add a **URL alias** for a term—a new feature of Drupal 7. This allows your users to easily view a list of all content that has been tagged by a particular term. The URL for the taxonomy term is independent from the URL for any nodes that the taxonomy has been attached to.

With the **RELATIONS** options, you can define relationships between the terms in the vocabulary.

Image styles

Now that images have been integrated directly into Drupal core, you can configure various image styles to control the size and appearance of images that are attached to the content. Similar functionality could be achieved in Drupal 6 by installing the Image and Image Cache modules. To access the image styles, click on **Configuration** from the administration toolbar and then click on **Image styles** in the **Media** section. You will receive a list of the styles that are currently defined:

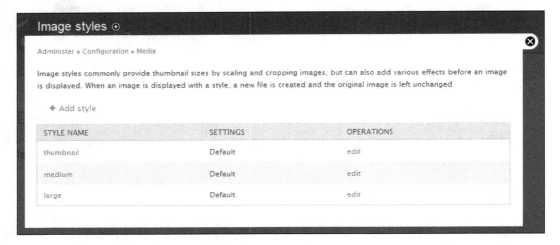

Drupal 7 ships with the **thumbnail**, **medium**, and **large** image styles by default. These set the maximum size of images as follows:

- Thumbnail—100 x 100px
- Medium—220 x 220px
- Large—640 x 640px

No changes are made to the original images other than resizing them, and the aspect ratio of the original image is preserved.

To create a new image style, click on the **Add style** link and give the style a name. The name must be machine readable and consist of letters, numbers, and underscores. After the style has been created, you can begin to apply effects. Each effect will be applied to the original image to create a new derivative image that is stored on the site. The available effects are:

Effect name	Description
Crop	Reduces the original image to a specific size by trimming any portion of the image that is outside of your desired boundaries.
Desaturate	Removes all color from the image converting it to a black and white image.
Resize	Resizes the image to a specific size. If the desired image does not have the same aspect ratio as the original image, the image will be stretched.
Rotate	Rotates the image around the center point of the image and adds a specified background color for any portion of the new image that is revealed by the rotation.
Scale	Resizes the image so it fits within the specified width and height without stretching it. The resulting image may not completely fill the specified width and height.

Each effect has its own additional configuration options, which can be modified to get exactly what you want. As you apply effects to your image style, a sample image will be updated to demonstrate the results of applying your style:

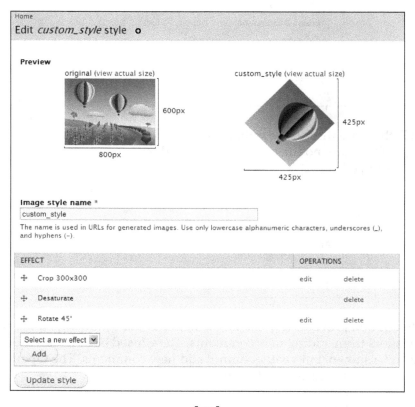

Experiment with various image effects and apply them in different orders until you achieve the look you want.

Comment changes

Drupal 7 greatly simplifies the comment system, especially for site visitors. Comments can be applied to any content type and can be modified for all instances of the content type by selecting the **Comment settings** tab while editing the content type:

In Drupal 7, there are three basic settings for how comments are handled for a content type. These are modified using the **Default comment setting for new content** drop-down list:

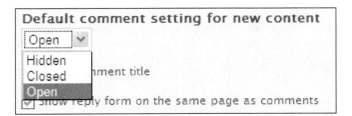

The **Hidden** option prevents any existing comments from showing on the site and prevents visitors from adding new comments. The **Closed** option allows existing comments to be shown, but visitors cannot add new comments. The **Open** option allows visitors to both see and add comments.

These basic settings can be overridden for each instance of the content type by accessing the comment settings when you add or edit the node.

You can also edit the display settings for comments within the content type. You can determine if messages should be threaded or displayed in a flat list. You can also set the number of comments to show at one time. In previous versions of Drupal, users could override some of these settings. However, that proved confusing and was removed in Drupal 7.

Removed functionality

Drupal 7 does not remove a significant amount of functionality related to content management. The only major removal was the Blog API that allowed editors to post content from desktop applications that support XML-RPC blog APIs. This functionality has been moved to a contributed module, which is available at `http://drupal.org/project/blogapi`.

Summary

In this chapter, we have reviewed some of the major changes and additions to Drupal 7 that relate to content management. We especially focused on the Field API, which replaced the CCK module that was available as a contributed module in Drupal 6. As we saw, Drupal 7 adds a great deal of new functionality that makes content management easier.

In the next chapter, we will be exploring changes in Drupal 7 that relate to administration of your Drupal 7 site.

4
Drupal 7 Administration

In the last chapter, we looked at changes to the Drupal 7 content management system. In this chapter, we will look into changes that have been made to the Administration interface in Drupal 7. In addition to discussing information about the new functionality that has been added to Drupal 7, we will also discuss areas where configuration options have been moved or renamed from Drupal 6 to Drupal 7. Some of the key changes include:

- The new administration toolbar so you can quickly access different areas of the site
- The administration overlay that allows you to administer your site without losing your place on the main site
- The new shortcut functionality that gives you immediate access to commonly-used commands
- Installation of modules and themes directly from your site
- The new administrator role that allows you to easily give administrators full access to the site without having to maintain permissions each time a new module is installed

At the end of this chapter, you should be able to navigate the new Drupal 7 administration interface, leverage the new administration features in Drupal 7, and easily find all your favorite features from Drupal 6.

New administration interface

The most obvious change for past Drupal administrators is the completely new administration interface. In addition to just looking different, the overall structure of the administration interface has been reworked. Although the new interface does take some getting used to if you have been working with Drupal for many years, the new interface is much more productive and presents information more clearly. Let's explore each section of the administration area before looking at each specific piece of functionality.

Administration toolbar

The Administration toolbar displays the major sections of the administration area and indicates which section is currently active.

Following is a brief description of each section:

- The **Dashboard** is a completely customizable page that allows you to set up your ideal interface for managing, monitoring, and maintaining your site.
- The **Content** section contains everything related to listing and adding content to your site. Key information includes lists of existing content as well as lists of existing comments. If you are using the Book module, your books are also listed here. The **Content** section also includes links to create new content.
- The **Structure** section has information related to organizing content on your site. Some of the subsections within the **Structure** section include: Blocks, Content types, Forums, Menus, Taxonomy, and more.
- The **Appearance** section allows you to select and configure the themes for your site.
- The **People** section allows you to manage your site's users and add new users to your site.
- The **Modules** section allows you to install and upgrade new modules as well as manage the modules that are already installed.

- The **Configuration** section gives you access to all of the administration options for many optional modules as well as standard options that do not fall into one of the other main sections. Depending on the modules you have installed, you can access a variety of subsections in the **Configuration** area including:

    ° **Regional and Language**: Settings related to dates, time zones, languages, and translations.

    ° **System**: Settings related to site information, actions, shortcuts, and statistics.

    ° **User Interface**: Settings related to Drupal's user interface.

    ° **Workflow**: This subsection contains tools to customize the process for creating, editing, and publishing content on the site.

    ° **Search and Metadata**: Settings related to paths, URLs, and searching.

    ° **People and Permissions**: Allows you to configure roles and permissions to determine what visitors can do on your site, and allows you to control who can access your site.

    ° **Development**: Miscellaneous settings related to logging, error reporting, performance, and monitoring.

    ° **Web Services**: Configuration for importing and exporting data as RSS information.

    ° **Media**: Settings related to the file system as well as images.

    ° **Content Authoring**: Allows you to modify options related to building content. By default, this includes the configuration of Text formats.

    As new modules are installed, new settings and new subsections may be added.

- The **Reports** section contains a variety of reports related to the operation of your website.

- The **Help** section, as its name implies, gives you access to online help related to the operation of your website.

- At the far right of the toolbar, the active user is displayed with a link to their user information. There is also a link to log out of the site.

- Finally, there is a link that allows you to open or close the shortcut bar.

Let's look at these sections in more detail. The changes within the **Content** and **Structure** sections were covered in the last chapter, so we will not cover them again here.

> Menu and Block functionality has not changed from Drupal 6. If you need a refresher course on these topics, you can refer to any Drupal 6 book, like *Drupal 6 Site Builder Solutions* that I authored, or any introductory Drupal 7 book.

Dashboard

Let's start by looking at the dashboard. The default dashboard is pretty spartan, as you can see in the following screenshot:

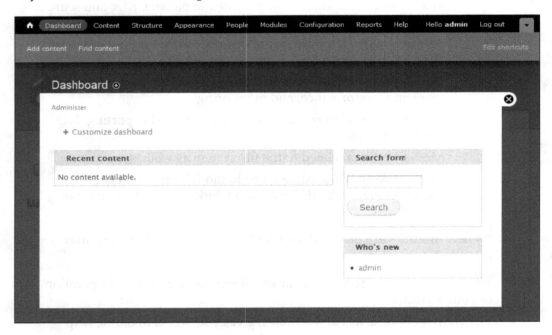

However, this spartan view belies the true power behind the dashboard. The default view contains two blocks—the management block, which contains a copy of the menus that make up the top toolbar, and a block to add new users to the site. Although this is an okay starting point, we can certainly make the dashboard more useful.

To customize the dashboard, click on the **Customize dashboard** link. This will open a new interface allowing you to modify the dashboard.

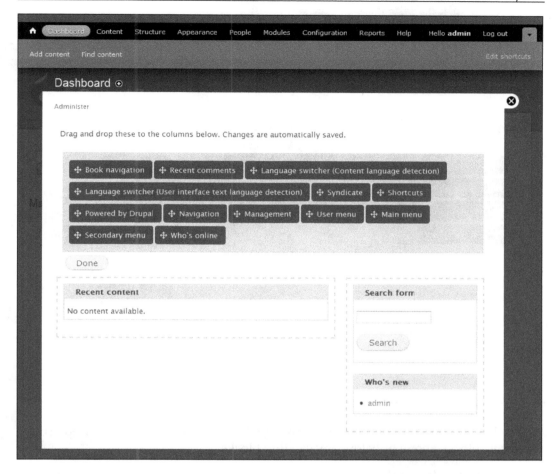

The dashboard is made up of two unequally sized regions. Each region can contain one or more blocks. Each region is outlined with dashed lines while you are customizing the dashboard. A list of all blocks that can be added to the dashboard are displayed above the regions.

To add a block to a region, drag it from the list of blocks to the region you want to insert it into.

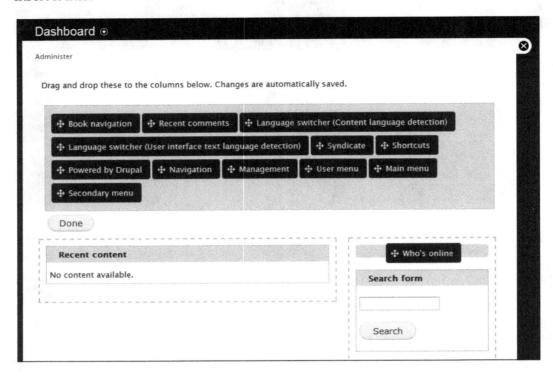

A gray bar will appear in the region showing where the block will be inserted. You can insert blocks above or below any existing blocks.

To remove a block, simply reverse the process by grabbing a block by its gray title bar and dragging it back to the list of blocks.

If you don't find a block that meets your needs in the existing list of blocks, you can create a custom block. For example, you could create a short menu of commonly-used links, or you could add blocks to return various statistics about your site. Let's build a quick block to display the current database size.

Start by clicking on the **Add block** link. You will be taken to the block creation page where you can enter information about the block.

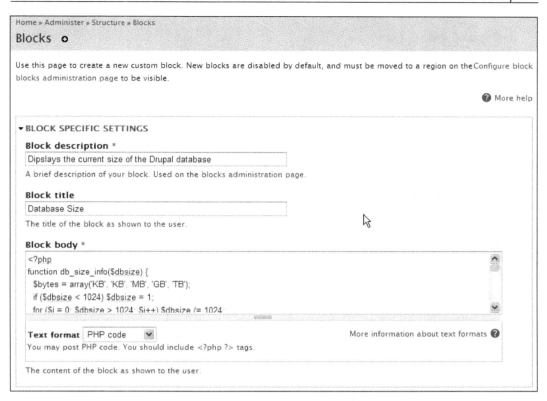

As you can see, we need to enter the title and description of the block as well as the body that controls the output of the block. In this case, we set the **Text format** to **PHP code** so we can query the database.

Here is the complete text of the block body. This code is based on a code snippet from the Drupal site, but it has been adjusted for Drupal 7. You can find the original Drupal 6 code at `http://drupal.org/node/100270`:

```php
<?php
function db_size_info($dbsize) {
  //Load the units of measure into an array
  $bytes = array('KB', 'KB', 'MB', 'GB', 'TB');
  //Reduce the size of the database to the correct scale by
  //dividing by 1024 until we reach a value between 1 and 1024
  if ($dbsize < 1024) $dbsize = 1;
  for ($i = 0; $dbsize > 1024; $i++) $dbsize /= 1024;
  //Now that the size has been reduced properly, setup the
  //return value and units.
  $db_size_info['size'] = ceil($dbsize);
```

```
    $db_size_info['type'] = $bytes[$i];
    return $db_size_info;
}

//Load statistics from the database
$rows = db_query("SHOW TABLE STATUS")->fetchAll();
//Loop through each row of data to calculate the total size
$dbssize = 0;
foreach ($rows as $row) {
    $dbssize += $row->data_length + $row->index_length;
}
//Print the raw number of bytes in the database
print "$dbssize bytes ";
//Calculate and print the normalized size of the database
$dbssize = db_size_info($dbssize);
print "({$dbssize['size']} {$dbssize['type']})";
?>
```

After you have entered the appropriate information into the block, click on the **Save block** button. The block will be created and added to the list of available blocks. To add it to your dashboard, simply drag it into one of the available regions. The resulting dashboard will appear similar to the following:

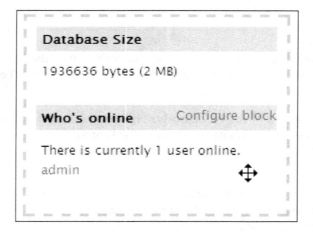

After you have finished modifying your database, click on the **Done** button to return to the regular view.

Overlay window

As you may have noticed in the previous screenshots, the administration pages no longer appear in their own page. Instead, they open in an overlay window, which appears on top of your normal site content as shown below:

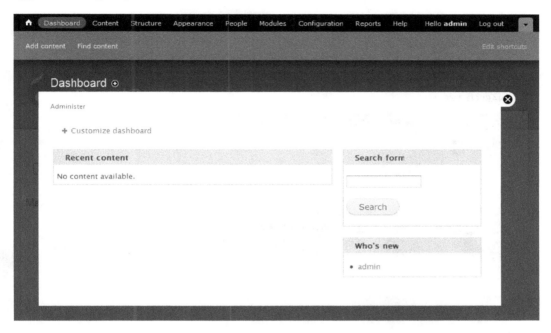

This allows you to easily return to your content after you have completed your administrative changes. You can close the overlay window by clicking on the **X** at the top right-hand side corner of the overlay panel.

Appearance section

The **Appearance** section gives you control over the themes installed on your site. When you first click on the **Appearance** link, you are taken to a list of themes that have been installed on the site, as shown in the following screenshot:

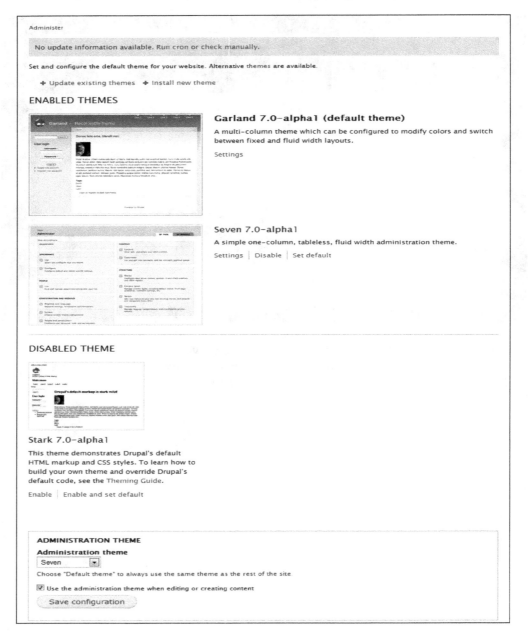

From this page, you can enable or disable themes and set the active theme, which is used when displaying content. The **Administration theme** drop down allows you to change the theme used when administering the site. This functionality is unchanged from Drupal 6. In Drupal 6, you could reach this functionality by selecting **Administer | Site building | Themes**. Clicking on the **Settings** link for an enabled theme allows you to change the display of various elements within the site, set logos and shortcut icons, and so on. The exact settings that are available depend on the theme being configured. This functionality matches the Drupal 6 functionality.

Installing and updating themes and modules

As you may have noticed on the list of available themes, there are links at the top of the page to **Update existing themes** and **Install new theme**. These are new features within Drupal 7, and they definitely make life easier for administrators. Let's start by looking into installing new themes and then we will review updating themes.

Installing new themes and modules

To start the installation process for a theme, click on the **Install new theme** link. This will display a form, as shown below, where you can install a theme or module:

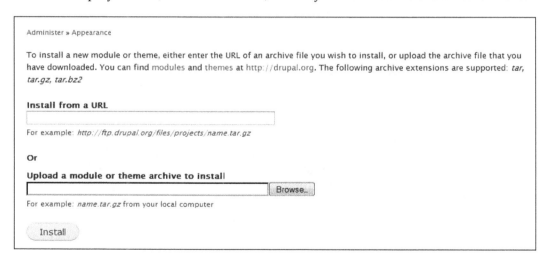

There are two different ways you can install a theme. You can either install the theme directly from the Drupal.org site to your local machine or you can upload a module that has either been downloaded from the Drupal.org site or built locally.

To install a theme from the `Drupal.org` site, you will first need to visit `Drupal.org` and find a theme that you want to use. After you have found a theme, visit its project page. Scroll down to the releases section and right click on the **Download** link:

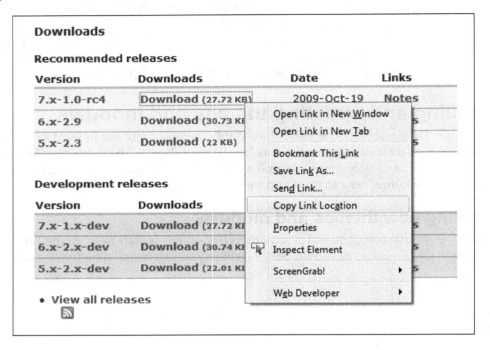

From the pop-up menu, select **Copy Link Location** if you are using Firefox or **Copy Shortcut** if you are using Internet Explorer. Other browsers will have similar options. This will copy the download path for the theme to your clipboard. Now switch back to your site and paste the link into the **Install from a URL** text box. After you have set the URL for the theme you want to install, click on the **Install** button. Drupal will automatically download the theme and install it onto your site. During this process, the status of the installation will be shown. After the installation is complete, you will receive a status page similar to the following:

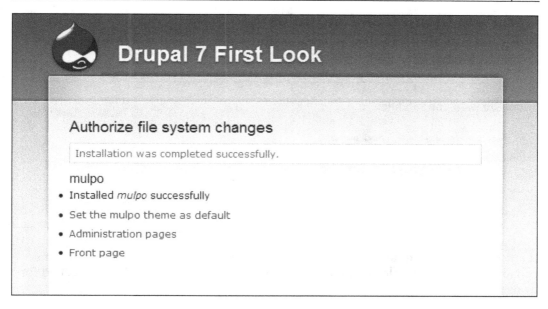

From this status page, you can set the new theme as your default theme or you can return to either the administration interface or your front page.

Installing from a downloaded package is similar to installing directly from a URL, with a few exceptions. After finding a theme that you like, download it to your local computer instead of simply copying the download link. You can then browse for the location of the module on your local computer. You will need to click on **Install** to start the installation process.

This functionality can also be used to install modules. The process is exactly the same as installing a theme and the status page is also similar.

Updating themes and modules

When you click on the **Update existing modules** link, Drupal will display a list of any modules that have updates available:

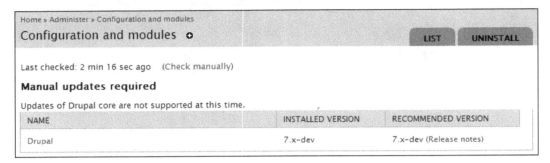

If any modules or themes have updates, you can install them from this page. You can also check for updates manually if the system has not automatically checked for updates recently.

People section

The **People** section allows you to view and manage the users within your site, and appears as follows:

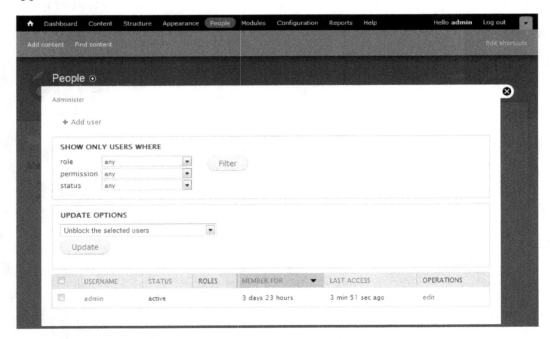

The functionality on this page is identical to the Drupal 6 functionality, which could be reached from **Administer | User Management | Users**. From this page, you can add new users administratively. You can also block users, completely cancel their account, or add and remove roles assigned to them.

Modules section

The **Modules** section allows you to determine which modules are active on your site and install new modules. All modules that have been installed on your site appear in a categorized list as shown in the following screenshot:

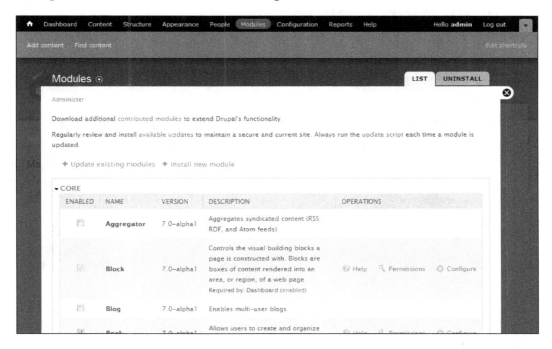

To enable the module, simply select the checkbox next to the module you want to enable and then click on **Save configuration** at the bottom of the page. To disable the module, simply deselect the checkbox and then click on **Save configuration**.

 Some modules have an uninstall process that cleans up the database or associated files. You can access the uninstall process by clicking on the **UNINSTALL** tab. Only uninstall a module if you are certain you will not use it in the future.

Drupal 7 also includes the ability to install a module directly from the Drupal.org website or from a downloaded installation package. The process for doing so is exactly the same as the process for installing themes, which we covered earlier in the chapter.

You can also access configuration settings for a module directly from the list of modules, change permissions for an individual module, and get additional help for a module. Any or all of these options may or may not be shown depending on the module in question.

Configuration section

The **Configuration** section contains the bulk of the settings you will need to properly set up your website. The main interface appears as follows:

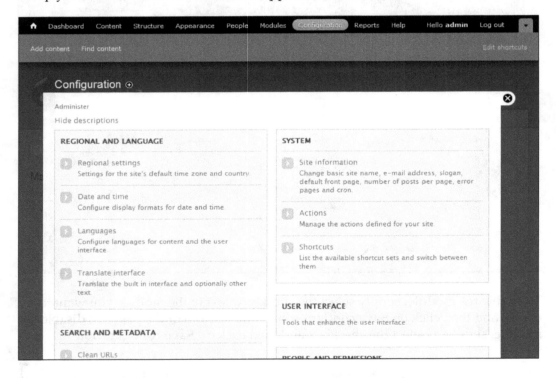

Because many different modules add their settings to this configuration page, the actual options which appear will vary depending on the modules you have activated for your site. For purposes of review, I have enabled all of the Drupal modules that are available in Drupal core.

Configuring settings

The majority of the settings are the same from Drupal 6 to Drupal 7. Let's look at each set of settings in Drupal 7. For each group of settings, we will identify the new Drupal 7 path and the old Drupal 6 path and menu descriptions. We will also provide a brief description of the settings contained within that section and list any settings that have been added or removed.

Regional and language

This section contains settings that you may need to change based on the geographic location of your site or the language(s) in which your site is written.

Regional settings

The details are as follows:

- **Drupal 7 path**: admin/config/regional/settings.
- **Drupal 6 menu location: Administer | Site configuration | Date and Time**.
- **Drupal 6 path**: admin/settings/date-time.
- **Description**: It contains settings for the default time zone for the site, whether or not users can set their own time zone, the default country, and the first day of the week.
- **New settings**: Drupal 7 adds the ability to remind users to set a time zone if they haven't set the time zone yet, and how the time zone should be handled when new users register on the site. Drupal 7 also adds the ability to set the default country for the site.

Date and time

The details are as follows:

- **Drupal 7 path**: admin/config/regional/date-time.
- **Drupal 6 menu location: Administer | Site configuration | Date and Time**.
- **Drupal 6 path**: admin/settings/date-time.
- **Description**: It contains settings related to the display of dates in various formats.
- **New settings**: Administrators that run multi-lingual sites will love all of the new settings related to dates and times. You can now format dates differently depending on which language a user has active. You can also define custom formats for date formatting. We will review all of this new functionality a little later in the chapter.

Language

The details are as follows:

- **Drupal 7 path**: `admin/config/regional/language`.
- **Drupal 6 menu location**: **Administer | Site configuration | Languages**.
- **Drupal 6 path**: `admin/settings/language`.
- **Description**: It allows configuration of which labels are available to site users for display on the site.
- **New settings**: Drupal 7 allows additional control over how the system detects which language should be used when displaying content to users. Drupal 7 also gives you the ability to control the language used to display labels independently from the language used to display content. We will review all of these changes in more detail later.

Translate interface

The details are as follows:

- **Drupal 7 path**: `admin/config/regional/translate`.
- **Drupal 6 menu location**: **Administer | Site building | Translate interface**.
- **Drupal 6 path**: `admin/build/translate`.
- **Description**: The translation settings allow you to translate information within the Drupal interface. To speed up the translation process, you can import translation files and you can also export information to be translated.
- **New settings**: The translation interface has been updated in a few locations to make it more compact and easier to use, but the actual functionality has not been changed from Drupal 6.

Search and metadata

The search and metadata section contains settings that change how visitors can search your site as well as settings that control how search engines see your site.

Clean URLs

The details are as follows:

- **Drupal 7 path**: `admin/config/search/clean-urls`
- **Drupal 6 menu location**: **Administer | Site configuration | Clean URLs**
- **Drupal 6 path**: `admin/settings/clean-urls`

- **Description**: Allows you to determine how URLs should be formed
- **New settings**: The overall look has changed slightly, but the functionality remains the same

Search settings

The search settings section contains settings related to how URLs appear on your site as well as giving you control over the actual search engine.

- **Drupal 7 path**: admin/config/search/settings.
- **Drupal 6 menu location: Administer | Site configuration | Search Settings**.
- **Drupal 6 path**: admin/settings/search.
- **Description**: Provides configuration options related to searching including the status of search indexing, the ability to index the site, determining how the site should be indexed, and how the indexing should work.
- **New settings**: Drupal 7 adds the ability to determine which search modules are active and allows you to enable or disable searching nodes and users independently. Drupal 7 also adds **Content is sticky at top of lists** and **Content is promoted to the front page** and removes **Recently posted** as content weighting factors.

URL aliases

- **Drupal 7 path**: admin/config/search/path
- **Drupal 6 menu location: Administer | Site building | URL aliases**
- **Drupal 6 path**: admin/build/path
- **Description**: Allows you to add aliases for paths in the system so that they can be more easily entered by visitors or to improve search engine rankings
- **New settings**: There have been no changes here from Drupal 6 to Drupal 7

Development

The development section gives you access to settings that allow you to get more information about the workings of your site as well as allowing you to monitor and configure performance-related settings. You can also access the automated test system from this section.

Logging and errors

The details are as follows:

- **Drupal 7 path**: admin/config/development/logging.
- **Drupal 6 menu location: Administer | Site configuration | Logging and alerts | Database Logging**.
- **Drupal 6 path**: admin/settings/logging/dblog.
- **Description**: Controls what information is logged to the database as well as how much data is kept at any one time.
- **New settings**: Drupal 7 adds the ability to log PHP messages to the Drupal log. The new options are shown in the following screenshot:

Maintenance mode

The details are as follows:

- **Drupal 7 path**: admin/config/development/maintenance
- **Drupal 6 menu location: Administer | Site configuration | Site maintenance**
- **Drupal 6 path**: admin/settings/site-maintenance
- **Description**: Allows you to close the site temporarily while running maintenance tasks or upgrading the site
- **New settings**: This functionality is unchanged from Drupal 6

Performance

The details are as follows:

- **Drupal 7 path**: admin/config/development/performance.
- **Drupal 6 menu location: Administer | Site configuration | Performance**.
- **Drupal 6 path**: admin/settings/performance.

- **Description**: Contains settings that can influence the overall performance of your site including caching information and combining files to reduce the amount of data that must be transmitted.

- **New settings**: Aggressive page caching was removed in Drupal 7. This was done to reduce confusion and to remove the chance of side effects occurring. The page compression setting has also been removed if the server already compresses requests. The page has also been reformatted to make it easier to understand and use.

Testing

The details are as follows:

- **Drupal 7 path**: `admin/config/development/testing`.
- **Drupal 6 menu location**: N/A.
- **Drupal 6 path**: N/A.
- **Description**: This link takes you to the automated testing system where you can run Drupal's built-in tests as well as any tests you have written for your own module. This functionality was not available in Drupal 6 except as the Simple Test contributed module.

Media section

This section of configuration options contains links to settings which control how images and files are treated within your site.

File system

The details are as follows:

- **Drupal 7 path**: `admin/config/media/file-system`.
- **Drupal 6 menu location**: **Administer | Site configuration | File system**.
- **Drupal 6 path**: `admin/settings/file-system`.
- **Description**: Gives you control over where files are stored on your server as well as how files are accessed.
- **New settings**: Drupal 7 now allows you to use both a public and private file system concurrently. Therefore, rather than selecting which method you would like to use, you simply select the default download method you wish to use.

Image styles

The details are as follows:

- **Drupal 7 path**: `admin/config/media/image-styles`.
- **Drupal 6 menu location**: N/A.
- **Drupal 6 path**: N/A.
- **Description**: Allows you to configure automatic resizing and processing of images that have been added to the site. This is all new functionality in Drupal 7, which we covered in detail in the last chapter.

Image toolkit

The details are as follows:

- **Drupal 7 path**: `admin/config/media/image-toolkit`.
- **Drupal 6 menu location**: **Administer | Site configuration | Image toolkit**.
- **Drupal 6 path**: `admin/settings/image-toolkit`.
- **Description**: Allows you to choose and configure image toolkits for the site. The default GD toolkit allows you to configure the image quality for JPEG images when the images are manipulated.
- **New settings**: This functionality has not changed from Drupal 6.

System section

The system section of settings gives you links to pages containing information about your site and allows you to configure information about the site as well as administration of the site.

Site information

The details are as follows:

- **Drupal 7 path**: `admin/config/system/site-information`.
- **Drupal 6 menu location**: **Administer | Site configuration | Site information**.
- **Drupal 6 path**: `admin/settings/site-information`.
- **Description**: Gives you the ability to configure basic information about your site including the site name, site e-mail, default home page, and so on.

- **New settings**: In Drupal 7, the Mission and Footer message fields have been removed. You can replicate these settings using custom blocks. Drupal 7 also adds the ability to configure pages to display when a page is not found (error 404), or when a user does not have access to functionality (error 403). This can be very useful if you want to send users to a login page or to a site map. Drupal 7 also adds a setting for the frequency to automatically run cron. We will discuss cron and the new cron system in more detail later in this chapter.

Actions

The details are as follows:

- **Drupal 7 path**: `admin/config/system/actions`.
- **Drupal 6 menu location: Administer | Site configuration | Actions.**
- **Drupal 6 path**: `admin/settings/actions`.
- **Description**: Allows you to build and manage actions within the system. Actions are specific individual tasks that the system performs. Actions can be run by other modules, including the Trigger module, when a specific circumstance arises. Actions can be either basic actions or complex actions that require configuration.
- **New settings**: The basic actions functionality has stayed the same in Drupal 7. However, there are several new actions that are provided in the default installation including:
    - Publish comment
    - Unpublish comment
    - Save comment
    - Publish content
    - Unpublish content

The names of actions related to nodes were also changed to refer to content rather than posts. We will cover changes to creating custom actions in Chapter 7.

Shortcuts

The details are as follows:

- **Drupal 7 path**: `admin/config/regional/system/shortcut`.
- **Drupal 6 menu location**: N/A.
- **Drupal 6 path**: N/A.

- **Description**: Allows you to build shortcuts for display in the new shortcuts bar.

- **New settings**: This is new Drupal 7 functionality. We will review this functionality in depth a little later in this chapter.

Statistics

The details are as follows:

- **Drupal 7 path**: admin/config/system/statistics.
- **Drupal 6 menu location**: **Administer | Reports | Access log settings**.
- **Drupal 6 path**: admin/reports/settings.
- **Description**: Allows you to control whether or not page visits are logged and how long log entries should be preserved. Also allows you to increment a counter when content is viewed.
- **New settings**: The display of these settings has been changed slightly, but the actual functionality remains the same.

People and permissions section

This section gives you access to settings related to site visitors, including what they can do on the site and what information the system stores about site visitors.

Account settings

The details are as follows:

- **Drupal 7 path**: admin/config/people/accounts.
- **Drupal 6 menu location**: **Administer | User management | User settings**.
- **Drupal 6 path**: admin/user/settings.
- **Description**: Allows you to configure how visitor registrations are handled on the site, automated e-mails that are sent to users, additional information about users, and more.
- **New settings**: The user accounts settings have changed substantially from Drupal 6. In Drupal 7, users can have fields and you can configure what happens when a user account is disabled. We will review these changes thoroughly in just a few pages.

Roles

The details are as follows:

- **Drupal 7 path**: `admin/config/people/roles`
- **Drupal 6 menu location**: **Administer | User management | Roles**
- **Drupal 6 path**: `admin/user/roles`
- **Description**: Lists active roles on the site and allows you to create new roles and assign permissions to roles
- **New settings**: This functionality remains the same in Drupal 7

Permissions

The details are as follows:

- **Drupal 7 path**: `admin/config/people/permissions`.
- **Drupal 6 menu location**: **Administer | User management | Permissions**.
- **Drupal 6 path**: `admin/user/permissions`.
- **Description**: Allows you to set permissions by role. All permissions are listed with all applicable roles.
- **New settings**: Additional descriptive information about each role has been added. However, the base functionality is the same as Drupal 6.

IP address blocking

The details are as follows:

- **Drupal 7 path**: `admin/config/people/ip-blocking`.
- **Drupal 6 menu location**: **Administer | User management | Access rules**.
- **Drupal 6 path**: `admin/user/rules`.
- **Description**: This page allows you to block certain computers based on IP address.

- **New settings**: The functionality of this page was migrated partially from the access rules in Drupal 6. In Drupal 7, you cannot block entire ranges of IP addresses. If you need to block a large number of IP addresses, you should block them either in an `.htaccess` file or in your firewall. The new page appears as follows:

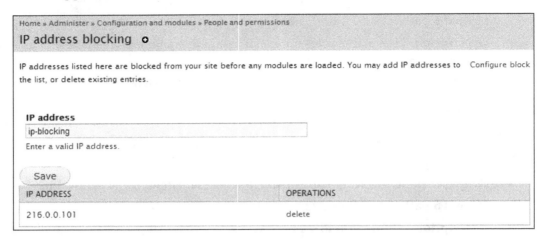

Profiles

The details are as follows:

- **Drupal 7 path**: `admin/config/people/profile`.
- **Drupal 6 menu location**: **Administer | User management | Profiles**.
- **Drupal 6 path**: `admin/user/profile`.
- **Description**: Allows you to add information to a user's profile page. Each field can be configured to control who has access to view the field. This allows sensitive information to be stored in such a way that modules and themes cannot access the information.
- **New settings**: This functionality has not changed from Drupal 6. However, if you do not need the additional access control that profiles provide, you should consider using fields to store the information.

Web Services section

This section gives you access to configuration options that allow you to control how your site sends and receives standardized content on the web.

Feed aggregator

The details are as follows:

- **Drupal 7 path**: admin/config/services/aggregator.
- **Drupal 6 menu location**: **Administer | Content management | Feed aggregator**.
- **Drupal 6 path**: admin/content/aggregator.
- **Description**: Allows you to add and categorize news feeds for display on your site.
- **New settings**: The aggregator settings are largely the same. However, the interface for listing the current categories and feeds includes links to create new categories and feeds. In Drupal 6, these links appeared as additional tabs. In Drupal 7, you can also configure the number of items to show in a recent news items block as well as the length to trim postings to when showing teasers. Finally, you can import OPML files to set up multiple feeds at once.

RSS publishing

The details are as follows:

- **Drupal 7 path**: admin/config/services/rss-publishing.
- **Drupal 6 menu location**: **Administer | Content management | RSS publishing**.
- **Drupal 6 path**: admin/content/rss-publishing.
- **Description**: Allows you to publish RSS feeds of your content so it can be used on other sites.
- **New settings**: Drupal 7 adds the ability to enter a description for your feed. All other functionality remains the same as Drupal 6.

Content Authoring section

This section contains settings that relate to how content is stored in Drupal and how it is presented to your site visitors.

Text formats

The details are as follows:

- **Drupal 7 path**: admin/config/content/formats.
- **Drupal 6 menu location**: **Administer | Site configuration | Input formats**.
- **Drupal 6 path**: admin/settings/filters.

- **Description**: Allows you to control what information can be entered into your site. You can allow specific tags or force the user to enter plain text only.

- **New settings**: Text formats have changed quite a bit from Drupal 6 Input formats. We reviewed all of the changes in the last chapter.

Shortcuts

The new Drupal 7 shortcut bar can be accessed by clicking on the drop-down arrow at the top right of the screen. The shortcut bar appears as follows by default:

By default, all users will share the same shortcuts. However, you can add additional sets of shortcuts. To configure shortcuts, click on the **Shortcuts** link from the **Configuration | System** section.

From this screen, you can switch between different shortcut sets (if you have more than one in the system), or you can create new shortcut sets. To create a new set of shortcuts, simply enter a new name and then click on the **Save configuration** button. You will now be taken to a screen where you can configure which shortcuts are in the set. The following screenshot shows the result of creating a new set of shortcuts called **Content Editor Shortcuts**:

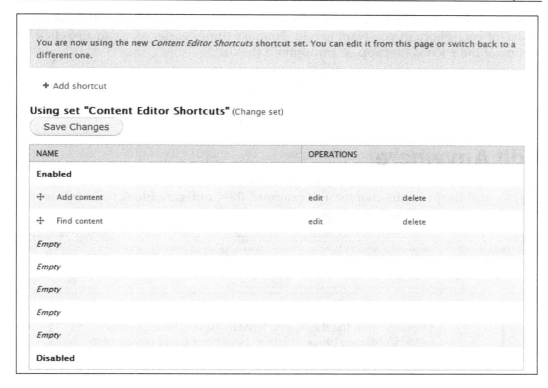

You can also reach the customization screen by clicking on the **Edit shortcuts** button at the top right-hand side corner of the shortcut bar. Each set of shortcuts can have up to eight links within it. To add a shortcut, click on the **Add shortcut** link. You will be prompted for a **Name** and **Path** for the shortcut:

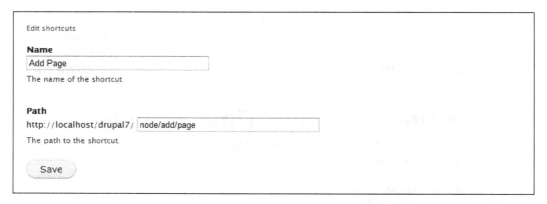

After you have entered the information to your satisfaction, click on the **Save** button.

This process can be a little more time consuming since you need to find the correct paths for each shortcut you want to add. To make things easier, you can also click on one of the + icons that appear throughout the site:

Edit Anywhere

You may have noticed a **Configure Block** link in several of the screenshots for this chapter and the previous chapter. For example, the **Configure block** link appears in the help text on the **Search settings** page:

The search engine maintains an index of words found in your site's content. To build and maintain this index, a Configure block correctly configured cron maintenance task is required. Indexing behavior can be adjusted using the settings below.

More help

> Depending on the theme you have installed, the appearance of the **Configure block** link may be different, and it may only appear if you mouse over a block.

When you place your mouse over the **Configure block** link, the extents of the block will be surrounded with a dashed line so you can easily tell what you are working with. If you click on the link, you will be taken to the edit page where you can make any needed changes to the block including changing visibility, changing titles, and so on.

This functionality is part of the new Edit Anywhere functionality that has been added to Drupal 7. In Drupal 6, a few themes, such as Zen, implemented similar functionality, but now you can take advantage of this functionality in any theme. Edit Anywhere is not just limited to blocks either. You can also edit menus directly.

Configuring Date and Time display

In the last section, we noted that the Date and Time configuration settings have changed from Drupal 6 to Drupal 7. Let's look at the changes in more detail.

The first tab on the **Date and time** settings page allows you to configure the date types that are available within the system. By default, there are three types available: **Long**, **Medium**, and **Short**.

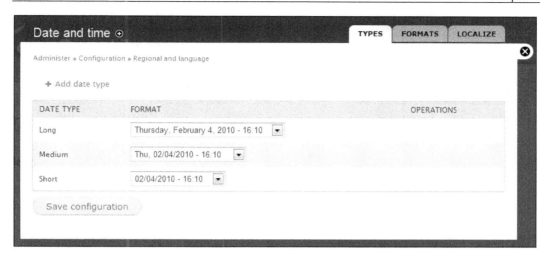

You can add a new date type by clicking on the **Add date type** link. Let's build an **Extra Long** date type. On the Add date type screen, simply enter the name of the type (Drupal will create an internal name for you) and select the **Date format** you want to use from the list of available formats.

Click on the **Add date type** button when you are satisfied with your selections.

If you can't find the format you want in the list, you can build your own date format. Click on the **FORMATS** tab and you will see a list of all the custom date formats that have been defined. By default, there aren't any.

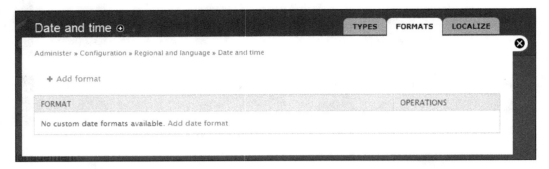

To add a new date format, click on the **Add format** or **Add date format** link. Let's build a date format that's very verbose.

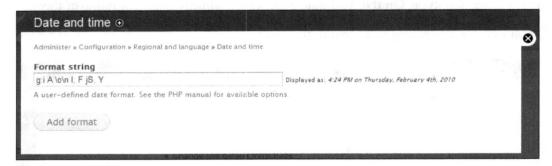

As you enter the format, Drupal will automatically display a sample representation of the format so you can verify that the format works as expected. After you are positive that the format works properly, click on the **Add format** button. Your new format will now be available for use on the Date types screen.

Also new to Drupal 7 is the ability to set date and time formats by language if you are running a multi-lingual site. This functionality is reached through the **LOCALIZE** tab.

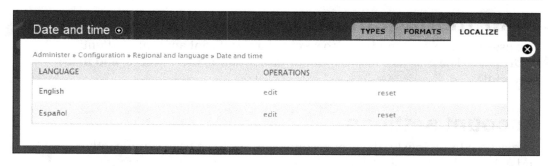

 The languages that are available on this page are defined in the Language page in the **Configuration** section. This page is available at http://yoursite.com/admin/config/regional/language.

To change the date formats for a particular language, simply select the **edit** link for the language. This takes you to a screen where you can override the default settings for a date type.

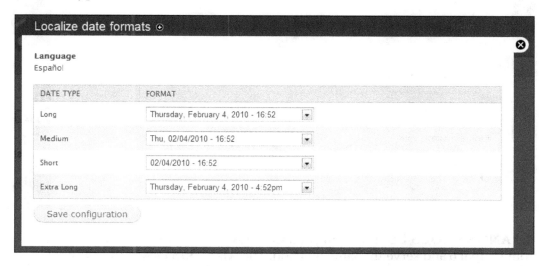

Typical changes here will include changing the order of the month and day and changing the format of the time to match the formatting that site visitors expect.

User management

The user management module also received a significant amount of attention in Drupal 7. The interface has been made easier to use, more secure, and more powerful.

Account settings

As discussed previously, the user account settings have been significantly revised and enhanced. Let's look at each section of the **Account settings** configuration section in detail:

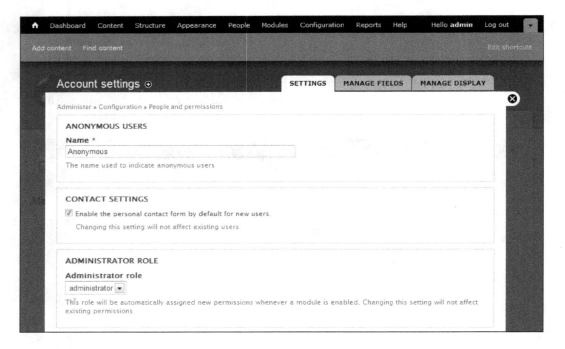

The **ANONYMOUS USERS** setting and **CONTACT SETTINGS** are carryovers from Drupal 6 and serve the same function. The **ADMINISTRATOR ROLE** setting is brand new in Drupal 7. This setting allows you to define a role that automatically has all permissions enabled for it. The Drupal installer creates an administrator account for you. You can also change this to any other role within the system here. When you change the administrator role, the new role will automatically have all new permissions assigned to it when modules are enabled. You can also set the **Administrator role** to **disabled**, which will prevent Drupal from automatically altering any roles.

If you change the administrator role, make sure to review the permissions for both the old role and the new role. Drupal does not modify any permissions when changing the administrator role, so you may need to enable or disable some permissions.

Let's look at the next section now, the **REGISTRATION AND CANCELLATION** settings:

REGISTRATION AND CANCELLATION

Who can register accounts?

○ Administrators only

◉ Visitors

○ Visitors, but administrator approval is required

☑ Require e-mail verification when a visitor creates an account.

New users will be required to validate their e-mail address prior to logging into the site, and will be assigned a system-generated password. With this setting disabled, users will be logged in immediately upon registering, and may select their own passwords during registration.

When cancelling a user account

◉ Disable the account and keep all content.

○ Disable the account and unpublish all content.

○ Delete the account and make all content belong to the *Anonymous* user.

○ Delete the account and all content.

Users with the *Select method for cancelling account* or *Administer users* permissions can override this default method.

The registration settings remain the same as in Drupal 6. However, the cancellation settings are brand new to Drupal 7. These settings allow you to determine what actions Drupal takes when a user cancels their account or when an administrator cancels a user's account. You have options to either disable or completely remove a user's account with a variety of options for dealing with any content the user created.

The ability for a user to cancel their own account is also new in Drupal 7. To allow a user to cancel their own account, you will need to give them permissions to do so.

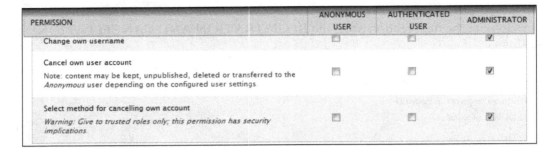

PERMISSION	ANONYMOUS USER	AUTHENTICATED USER	ADMINISTRATOR
Change own username	☐	☐	☑
Cancel own user account Note: content may be kept, unpublished, deleted or transferred to the *Anonymous* user depending on the configured user settings.	☐	☐	☑
Select method for cancelling own account *Warning: Give to trusted roles only; this permission has security implications.*	☐	☐	☑

The relevant permissions are **Cancel own user account** and **Select method for cancelling own account**. Depending on your site, you may want to enable these permissions for authenticated users.

The next section within the Account settings is **PERSONALIZATION**:

These settings remain unchanged from Drupal 6 other than a few default settings having changed. For example, user pictures are enabled by default and the default maximum size of pictures has been increased.

The final section is the **E-mails** section. This section has been reformatted so it is much more compact and easier to read:

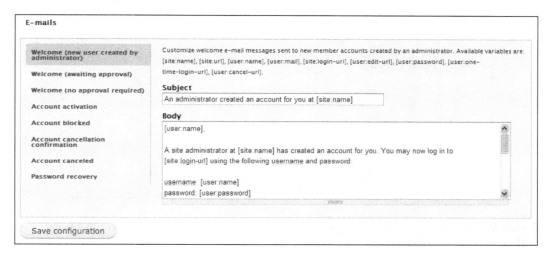

New settings for generating e-mails to users when their account is canceled or about to be canceled have been added. The remaining e-mails remain the same.

User fields

Similar to content types, comments, and taxonomies, users can also have fields in Drupal 7. This functionality is similar to the Drupal 6 Profile module. However, fields do not have the same level of control over the visibility of individual fields that the Profile module gives. In general, you should use fields unless you need strict control over who can access the data.

Fields are added in exactly the same manner used to add them to content types, comments, taxonomies, and so on.

Password strength meter

When new users are created in the system either by an administrator or by a site visitor, a new **Password strength** meter is displayed to help users ensure that their password cannot be guessed easily:

```
Password *
[ ••• ]                              Password strength:        Weak

Confirm password *
[                    ]

  ┌────────────────────────────────────────────────────────┐
  │ To make your password stronger:                          │
  │ Make it at least 6 characters                            │
  │ Add uppercase letters                                    │
  │ Add numbers                                              │
  │ Add punctuation                                          │
  └────────────────────────────────────────────────────────┘

Provide a password for the new account in both fields.
```

As the user enters their desired password, the system will analyze the password and suggest ways to make it more difficult to guess.

Login rate limitations

Drupal core now includes a mechanism to help protect against brute force login attempts. The system will prevent users from logging in if they provide an incorrect password for their username five times in six hours. The system will also prevent any IP address from logging in if that IP address is responsible for 50 failed login attempts in one hour. If these criteria are met, the user will be informed that their login attempt has failed and they will be taken to a page where they can request a new password.

The settings for the login rate limiter were carefully chosen and should work for a majority of sites. However, if your users are having problems logging in or if you find yourself wanting to lower these thresholds, you can modify the following settings: `user_failed_login_ip_limit`, `user_failed_login_ip_window`, `user_failed_login_identifier_uid_only`, `flood_control_user_identifier`, `user_failed_login_user_limit`, and `user_failed_login_user_window`.

There is no administration interface for these settings so you will need to set them via a custom module or set them directly in your database. You can also add the custom Flood control module that exposes some of these settings (`http://drupal.org/project/flood_control`).

Search

Administrators and visitors to multi-lingual sites will be pleased to see that the search interface now allows searching specific languages on a site:

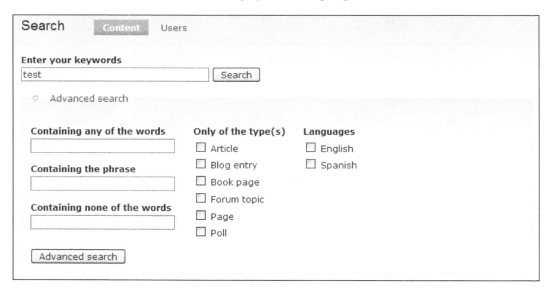

As you can see above, the advanced search page contains a section for the languages to search. If no languages are selected, all languages will be searched.

The advanced search screen is only available if you have granted a user the **Use advanced search** permission.

Changes to the cron system

A common problem for new administrators is setting up cron correctly. Depending on your host and operating system, you may not have access to cron or it may be difficult to configure. Thankfully, Drupal 7 provides automated cron functionality so that cron is always running after an installation.

The settings for cron can be found in the **Site information** settings within the **Configuration** section:

Automatically run cron

3 hours ▼

When enabled, the site will check whether cron has been run in the configured interval and automatically run it upon the next page request. For more information visit the status report page.

The automated cron system is triggered when a user visits your site after the cron interval has elapsed. The automated cron system is designed to work asynchronously in order to prevent performance from being impacted for the user who triggers cron. If you used Poormanscron (http://drupal.org/project/poormanscron) in Drupal 6, you will be very familiar with the Drupal 7 version.

If you prefer to use a true Unix-based cron system, simply change this setting to **Never** and then configure cron to run as usual.

Protection from unauthorized access

The new Drupal 7 cron also adds protection from being run by unauthorized users. By default, cron can only be run by the first user or if you provide a special key to cron. This key is automatically generated by the automated cron system and returned to the client when cron needs to be triggered. After the key is used, it is reset to a new value.

Reports

The **Reports** section contains reports about your site and the content within it. All of the reports from Drupal 6 have been carried forward and a new **Field list** report has been added. The full list of reports is as follows:

Administer

Recent log entries
View events that have recently been logged.

Field list
Overview of fields on all object types.

Recent hits
View pages that have recently been visited.

Top 'access denied' errors
View 'access denied' errors (403s).

Top 'page not found' errors
View 'page not found' errors (404s).

Top referrers
View top referrers.

Top search phrases
View most popular search phrases.

Top pages
View pages that have been hit frequently.

Top visitors
View visitors that hit many pages.

Available updates
Get a status report about available updates for your installed modules and themes.

Status report
Get a status report about your site's operation and any detected problems.

Field list report

The **Field list** report shows you a list of all the standard and custom fields within your site with a list of all the places where each field is used:

Home » Administer » Reports

Field list ✪

This list shows all fields currently in use for easy reference.   Configure block

FIELD NAME	FIELD TYPE	USED IN
body	Long text and summary	Article, Blog entry, Book page, Forum topic, Page
field_image	Image	Article
taxonomy_forums	Taxonomy term	Forum topic
taxonomy_tags	Taxonomy term	Article
title	Text	Article, Blog entry, Book page, Forum topic, Page, Poll

This report is very useful when you want to audit the fields on your site and determine the possible ramifications of changing field settings or deleting a field.

Summary

In this chapter we thoroughly reviewed the new administration functionality in Drupal 7 and we mapped the Drupal 6 functionality that carried forward into Drupal 7 so you can easily find your favorite features.

In the next chapter we will explore ways to enhance both content management and the administration of your site using some of the new contributed modules in Drupal 7. We will also discuss some of the key differences between the Drupal 6 version of these modules and the Drupal 7 version. Finally, where applicable, we will discuss upgrading modules from Drupal 6 to Drupal 7.

5
Drupal 7 for Themers

In previous chapters, we have explored many of the changes introduced in Drupal 7 to make life easier for system administrators and content editors. In this chapter, we will begin looking at changes to make Drupal 7 sites look better and to make life easier for themers. Specifically, we will look into changes to:

- Server-side PHP files, which make up the theme and generate the HTML for presentation to the end user
- CSS files, elements, and IDs that make changing the style of the site possible
- JavaScript functionality that makes your site more dynamic and responsive

After we cover these topics, we will look at all of the changes to the theme API functions including a detailed look at all of the new methods as well as the methods that have been deleted. For the deleted methods, we will describe what functionality should be used to replace the old functionality.

We will also cover all of the changes you need to make to your existing themes in order to upgrade them from version 6 to version 7.

Template changes

Drupal 7 makes several modifications to the files needed to build a theme. These changes are designed to make building themes easier and to make execution faster.

A high quality Drupal theme needs several key files to function properly including a `.info` file, a `page.tpl.php` file, a `template.php` file, `.css` files, and JavaScript files. Let's look at each of these files in detail. The files for a template are all placed in a directory named for the theme located in the `sites/all/themes` directory. For example, if we were creating a new theme called Drupal 7 Rocks, we would start by building a directory called `drupal_7_rocks` within the sites/all/themes directory. Now we can start to add files to that directory to start building the theme.

Everything there is to know about .info files

The .info file tells Drupal about your theme including the name of the theme, a description for the theme, and the .css and JavaScript files that make up the theme. Let's look at the Garland.info file that is distributed with the Drupal core:

```
$Id: garland.info,v 1.9 2009/12/01 15:57:40 webchick Exp $
name = Garland
description = A multi-column theme which can be configured to modify
colors and switch between fixed and fluid width layouts.
package = Core
version = VERSION
core = 7.x
engine = phptemplate
stylesheets[all][] = style.css
stylesheets[print][] = print.css
settings[garland_width] = fluid

; Information added by drupal.org packaging script on 2009-12-10
version = "7.x-dev"
core = "7.x"
project = "drupal"
datestamp = "1260403512"
```

The format of the .info file is very similar to the .info files we saw in Chapter 4 while we were looking at installation profiles. Many of the variables are also the same. When generating a custom theme, you will need to prefix the .info file with the name of the theme. In our example, the .info file would be named drupal_7_rocks.info.

The file again begins with the $Id line that is automatically generated by the version control system. The .info file then proceeds with the name and description of the theme. This information is displayed on the list of themes within the administration interface. The package can be used to define a grouping of themes. This is not currently used in the interface. The version and core lines identify compatibility of the theme with Drupal core. The engine defines which theme engine the theme will use. In nearly all cases, you will use the phptemplate template engine. Additional information about other template engines that are Drupal compatible can be found at http://drupal.org/node/176129.

After all of the preliminary variables, we finally reach the good part of the .info file. The definition of the stylesheets and settings:

```
stylesheets[all][] = style.css
stylesheets[print][] = print.css
settings[garland_width] = fluid
```

This is also the first deviation from Drupal 6. Drupal 6 would automatically include a `style.css`, `scripts.js`, and `screenshot.png` even if they were not defined in the `.info` file and did not exist. This led to major problems when subthemes did not define these files. Therefore, Drupal 7 removed this ability.

You can also define screenshots, regions, features, scripts, stylesheets, and the minimum required version of PHP in the `.info` file. For more information, see `http://drupal.org/node/171205`.

html.tpl.php

Drupal 7 adds a new template to the rendering process, the `html.tpl.php` file, which is responsible for displaying a basic header and setting up the body of the page. However, it does not render any actual page content or control the layout of pages. In most cases, the overall structure of the HTML page does not change from theme to theme. Therefore, most themes will not override the `html.tpl.php` file. The default file is located in `modules/system`. If you want to override the overall layout, you can copy the default `html.tpl.php` file to your theme and make any changes needed. Let's look at the default file:

```php
<?php
// $Id: html.tpl.php,v 1.3 2009/11/16 05:34:24 webchick Exp $

/**
 * @file
 * Default theme implementation to display the basic html structure of
 * a single Drupal page.
 *
 * Variables:
 * - $css: An array of CSS files for the current page.
 * - $language: (object) The language the site is being displayed in.
 *   $language->language contains its textual representation.
 *   $language->dir contains the language direction. It will either be
 *   'ltr' or 'rtl'.
 * - $rdf_namespaces: All the RDF namespace prefixes used in the HTML
 *   document.
 * - $grddl_profile: A GRDDL profile allowing agents to extract the
 *   RDF data.
 * - $head_title: A modified version of the page title, for use in the
 *   TITLE tag.
 * - $head: Markup for the HEAD section (including meta tags, keyword
 *   tags, and so on).
```

```
 * - $styles: Style tags necessary to import all CSS files for the
 *   page.
 * - $scripts: Script tags necessary to load the JavaScript files and
 *   settings for the page.
 * - $page_top: Initial markup from any modules that have altered the
 *   page. This variable should always be output first, before all
 *   other dynamic content.
 * - $page: The rendered page content.
 * - $page_bottom: Final closing markup from any modules that have
 *   altered the page. This variable should always be output last,
 *   after all other dynamic content.
 * - $classes String of classes that can be used to style contextually
 *   through CSS.
 *
 * @see template_preprocess()
 * @see template_preprocess_html()
 * @see template_process()
 */
?><!DOCTYPE html PUBLIC "-//W3C//DTD XHTML+RDFa 1.0//EN"
  "http://www.w3.org/MarkUp/DTD/xhtml-rdfa-1.dtd">
<html xmlns="http://www.w3.org/1999/xhtml" xml:lang="<?php print
$language->language; ?>" version="XHTML+RDFa 1.0" dir="<?php print
$language->dir; ?>"
  <?php print $rdf_namespaces; ?>>

<head profile="<?php print $grddl_profile; ?>">
  <?php print $head; ?>
  <title><?php print $head_title; ?></title>
  <?php print $styles; ?>
  <?php print $scripts; ?>
</head>
<body class="<?php print $classes; ?>" <?php print $attributes;?>>
  <div id="skip-link">
    <a href="#main-content"><?php print t('Skip to main content');
    ?></a>
  </div>
  <?php print $page_top; ?>
  <?php print $page; ?>
  <?php print $page_bottom; ?>
</body>
</html>
```

The beginning comments that start at the line containing /** and ending with the line containing */ give background information on how to use the file as well as the information that is available within the file. Let's look at the meat of the file, which starts with <!DOCTYPE:

```
?><!DOCTYPE html PUBLIC "-//W3C//DTD XHTML+RDFa 1.0//EN"
  "http://www.w3.org/MarkUp/DTD/xhtml-rdfa-1.dtd">
```

The DOCTYPE statement tells browsers what version of HTML your site is using and how the browser should interpret the code. By default, Drupal uses XHTML with RDF.

Next comes the opening statement for the HTML document. This defines the namespace for the document, the language that the document is written in, and additional information about the RDF data. The following lines of code:

```
<html xmlns="http://www.w3.org/1999/xhtml" xml:lang="<?php print
$language->language; ?>" version="XHTML+RDFa 1.0" dir="<?php print
$language->dir; ?>"
  <?php print $rdf_namespaces; ?>>
```

will translate to a header that appears similar to the following in the final page:

```
<html xmlns="http://www.w3.org/1999/xhtml" xml:lang="en"
version="XHTML+RDFa 1.0" dir="ltr"
  xmlns:admin="http://webns.net/mvcb/"
  xmlns:content="http://purl.org/rss/1.0/modules/content/"
  xmlns:dc="http://purl.org/dc/terms/"
  xmlns:foaf="http://xmlns.com/foaf/0.1/"
  xmlns:owl="http://www.w3.org/2002/07/owl#"
  xmlns:rdf="http://www.w3.org/1999/02/22-rdf-syntax-ns#"
  xmlns:rdfs="http://www.w3.org/2000/01/rdf-schema#"
  xmlns:rss="http://purl.org/rss/1.0/"
  xmlns:tags="http://www.holygoat.co.uk/owl/redwood/0.1/tags/"
  xmlns:sioc="http://rdfs.org/sioc/ns#"
  xmlns:sioct="http://rdfs.org/sioc/types#"
  xmlns:ctag="http://commontag.org/ns#"
  xmlns:skos="http://www.w3.org/2004/02/skos/core#"
  xmlns:xsd="http://www.w3.org/2001/XMLSchema#">
```

Next, the template prints header information for the document:

```
<head profile="<?php print $grddl_profile; ?>">
  <?php print $head; ?>
  <title><?php print $head_title; ?></title>
  <?php print $styles; ?>
  <?php print $scripts; ?>
</head>
```

The document head contains links to CSS stylesheets and JavaScript code as well as the title of the page. Other information may also be included in the $head variable depending on the configuration of the site.

The remaining portion of the template starts the body of the document and then prints the content that is generated using the page.tpl.php template:

```
<body class="<?php print $classes; ?>" <?php print $attributes;?>>
  <div id="skip-link">
    <a href="#main-content"><?php print t('Skip to main content');
    ?></a>
  </div>
  <?php print $page_top; ?>
  <?php print $page; ?>
  <?php print $page_bottom; ?>
</body>
```

Rendering the entire page with page.tpl.php

The page.tpl.php file contains the logic to render all of the regions within a page, which are rendered by other templates in the system. The default file is located in the /modules/system directory, but like any template, it can be overridden by copying it to your theme directory. The structure of the file is very similar to the Drupal 6 template. However, there are some important differences. Let's go through the new default template file in detail pointing out key difference as we go:

```
<?php
// $Id: page.tpl.php,v 1.39 2009/11/20 04:20:38 webchick Exp $

/**
 * @file
 * Default theme implementation to display a single Drupal page.
 *
 * Available variables:
 *
 * General utility variables:
 * - $base_path: The base URL path of the Drupal installation. At the
     very least, this will always default to /.
 * - $directory: The directory the template is located in, e.g.
     modules/system or themes/garland.
 * - $is_front: TRUE if the current page is the front page.
 * - $logged_in: TRUE if the user is registered and signed in.
```

```
 *  - $is_admin: TRUE if the user has permission to access
      administration pages.
 *
 * Site identity:
 *  - $front_page: The URL of the front page. Use this instead of
      $base_path, when linking to the front page. This includes the
      language domain or prefix.
 *  - $logo: The path to the logo image, as defined in theme
      configuration.
 *  - $site_name: The name of the site, empty when display has been
      disabled in theme settings.
 *  - $site_slogan: The slogan of the site, empty when display has been
      disabled in theme settings.
 *
 * Navigation:
 *  - $main_menu (array): An array containing the Main menu links for
      the site, if they have been configured.
 *  - $secondary_menu (array): An array containing the Secondary menu
      links for the site, if they have been configured.
 *  - $breadcrumb: The breadcrumb trail for the current page.
 *
 * Page content (in order of occurrence in the default page.tpl.php):
 *  - $title: The page title, for use in the actual HTML content.
 *  - $messages: HTML for status and error messages. Should be
      displayed prominently.
 *  - $tabs (array): Tabs linking to any sub-pages beneath the current
      page (e.g., the view and edit tabs when displaying a node).
 *  - $action_links (array): Actions local to the page, such as 'Add
      menu' on the menu administration interface.
 *  - $feed_icons: A string of all feed icons for the current page.
 *  - $node: The node object, if there is an automatically-loaded node
 *    associated with the page, and the node ID is the second argument
 *    in the page's path (e.g. node/12345 and node/12345/revisions, but
      not comment/reply/12345).
 *
 * Regions:
 *  - $page['help']: Dynamic help text, mostly for admin pages.
 *  - $page['highlight']: Items for the highlighted content region.
 *  - $page['content']: The main content of the current page.
 *  - $page['sidebar_first']: Items for the first sidebar.
 *  - $page['sidebar_second']: Items for the second sidebar.
 *  - $page['header']: Items for the header region.
 *  - $page['footer']: Items for the footer region.
 *
```

```
 * @see template_preprocess()
 * @see template_preprocess_page()
 * @see template_process()
 */
?>
  <div id="page-wrapper"><div id="page">
    <div id="header"><div class="section clearfix">
      <?php if ($logo): ?>
        <a href="<?php print $front_page; ?>" title="<?php print
        t('Home'); ?>" rel="home" id="logo">
          <img src="<?php print $logo; ?>" alt="<?php print t('Home');
          ?>" />
        </a>
      <?php endif; ?>
      <?php if ($site_name || $site_slogan): ?>
        <div id="name-and-slogan">
          <?php if ($site_name): ?>
            <?php if ($title): ?>
              <div id="site-name"><strong>
                <a href="<?php print $front_page; ?>" title="<?php
                print t('Home'); ?>" rel="home"><span><?php print
                $site_name; ?></span></a>
              </strong></div>
            <?php else: /* Use h1 when the content title is empty */
            ?>
              <h1 id="site-name">
                <a href="<?php print $front_page; ?>" title="<?php
                print t('Home'); ?>" rel="home"><span><?php print
                $site_name; ?></span></a>
              </h1>
            <?php endif; ?>
          <?php endif; ?>
          <?php if ($site_slogan): ?>
            <div id="site-slogan"><?php print $site_slogan; ?></div>
          <?php endif; ?>
        </div> <!-- /#name-and-slogan -->
      <?php endif; ?>
      <?php print render($page['header']); ?>
    </div></div> <!-- /.section, /#header -->
    <?php if ($main_menu): ?>
      <div id="navigation"><div class="section">
```

```php
  <?php print theme('links', array('links' => $main_menu,
  'attributes' => array('id' => 'main-menu',
  'class' => array('links', 'clearfix')),
  'heading' => t('Main menu'))); ?>
  </div></div> <!-- /.section, /#navigation -->
<?php endif; ?>

<?php if ($breadcrumb): ?>
  <div id="breadcrumb"><?php print $breadcrumb; ?></div>
<?php endif; ?>

<?php print $messages; ?>

<div id="main-wrapper"><div id="main" class="clearfix">

  <div id="content" class="column"><div class="section">
    <?php if ($page['highlight']): ?>
    <div id="highlight">
    <?php print render($page['highlight']); ?>
    </div><?php endif; ?>
    <a name="main-content" id="main-content"></a>
    <?php if ($title): ?>
    <h1 class="title" id="page-title"><?php print $title; ?>
    </h1><?php endif; ?>
    <?php if ($tabs): ?>
    <div class="tabs"><?php print render($tabs); ?>
    </div><?php endif; ?>
    <?php print render($page['help']); ?>
    <?php if ($action_links): ?>
    <ul class="action-links"><?php print render($action_links);
    ?></ul><?php endif; ?>
    <?php print render($page['content']); ?>
    <?php print $feed_icons; ?>
  </div></div> <!-- /.section, /#content -->

  <?php if ($page['sidebar_first']): ?>
    <div id="sidebar-first" class="column sidebar">
    <div class="section">
      <?php print render($page['sidebar_first']); ?>
    </div></div> <!-- /.section, /#sidebar-first -->
  <?php endif; ?>

  <?php if ($page['sidebar_second']): ?>
    <div id="sidebar-second" class="column sidebar">
    <div class="section">
      <?php print render($page['sidebar_second']); ?>
    </div></div> <!-- /.section, /#sidebar-second -->
  <?php endif; ?>
```

```
</div></div> <!-- /#main, /#main-wrapper -->

<div id="footer"><div class="section">
  <?php print theme('links', array('links' => $secondary_
  menu, 'attributes' => array('id' => 'secondary-menu',
  'class' => array('links', 'clearfix')),
  'heading' => t('Secondary menu'))); ?>
  <?php print render($page['footer']); ?>
</div></div> <!-- /.section, /#footer -->

</div></div> <!-- /#page, /#page-wrapper
```

Again, the template starts with a lengthy comment section describing the file and the variables that are available within the template. Many of the variables that are available have changed including:

- Several variables have been removed from the page template since they are now used in `html.tpl.php`. These include the `$css`, `$language`, `$head_title`, `$styles`, `$scripts`, and `$body_classes` variables.

- There are also several variables that are now rendered as blocks. These include `$mission`, `$search_box`, `$feed_icons`, and `$footer_message`.

- The menu variables have also been renamed from `$primary_links` and `$secondary_links` to `$main_menu` and `$secondary_menu` respectively, which are much more understandable.

- Finally, several variables have been moved into the `$page` array, which now holds the data that has been rendered by the region template. The actual regions that are available is controlled by the `.info` file for the theme. By default, the page includes the help, highlight, content, sidebar_first, sidebar_second, header, and footer regions.

The most obvious change to the page template file is that it no longer renders the entire page. As we discussed earlier, the `html.tpl.php` file is now responsible for rendering the header as well as the body container for the page.

The page template now starts with several containers to make the application of CSS styling easier:

```
<div id="page-wrapper"><div id="page">
```

The template now renders the header of the page including the logo, site name, and site-slogan:

```
<div id="header"><div class="section clearfix">

    <?php if ($logo): ?>
      <a href="<?php print $front_page; ?>" title="<?php print
      t('Home'); ?>" rel="home" id="logo">
```

```
      <img src="<?php print $logo; ?>" alt="<?php print t('Home');
      ?>" />
    </a>
  <?php endif; ?>

  <?php if ($site_name || $site_slogan): ?>
    <div id="name-and-slogan">
      <?php if ($site_name): ?>
        <?php if ($title): ?>
          <div id="site-name"><strong>
          <a href="<?php print $front_page; ?>" title="<?php print
          t('Home'); ?>" rel="home"><span><?php print $site_name;
          ?>
          </span></a>
          </strong></div>
        <?php else: /* Use h1 when the content title is empty */
        ?>
          <h1 id="site-name">
            <a href="<?php print $front_page; ?>"
            title="<?php print t('Home'); ?>"
            rel="home"><span><?php print $site_name; ?></span></a>
          </h1>
        <?php endif; ?>
      <?php endif; ?>

      <?php if ($site_slogan): ?>
        <div id="site-slogan"><?php print $site_slogan; ?></div>
      <?php endif; ?>
    </div> <!-- /#name-and-slogan -->
  <?php endif; ?>

  <?php print render($page['header']); ?>

</div></div> <!-- /.section, /#header -->
```

This code is very similar to Drupal 6 except that it adds more error checking when displaying common elements. The code also uses the new region template to render the `$page['header']` variable rather than rendering the `$header` variable and `$search_box`. Drupal 7 also adds a section class around each key area of the page to make styling easier.

Next, the template prints the main navigation elements including the main menu and breadcrumbs if these elements are sent:

```
  <?php if ($main_menu): ?>
    <div id="navigation"><div class="section">
      <?php print theme('links', array('links' => $main_menu,
      'attributes' => array('id' => 'main-menu',
      'class' => array('links', 'clearfix')),
```

```
      'heading' => t('Main menu'))); ?>
    </div></div> <!-- /.section, #navigation -->
  <?php endif; ?>
  <?php if ($breadcrumb): ?>
    <div id="breadcrumb"><?php print $breadcrumb; ?></div>
  <?php endif; ?>
```

The order of these elements is somewhat different from Drupal 6, but the basic code to render each element is largely the same.

Next, the template prints any messages from the system.

```
  <?php print $messages; ?>
```

The next key section of the template is the main content. This includes the main column as well as any sidebar regions that have been defined by the theme. If you are creating your own theme, you will most likely be making most of your changes in this area. The full code of this section is as follows:

```
<div id="main-wrapper"><div id="main" class="clearfix">
  <div id="content" class="column"><div class="section">
    <?php if ($page['highlight']): ?><div id="highlight">
    <?php print render($page['highlight']); ?></div><?php endif; ?>
    <a name="main-content" id="main-content"></a>
    <?php if ($title): ?><h1 class="title" id="page-title">
    <?php print $title; ?></h1><?php endif; ?>
    <?php if ($tabs): ?><div class="tabs">
    <?php print render($tabs); ?></div><?php endif; ?>
    <?php print render($page['help']); ?>
    <?php if ($action_links): ?><ul class="action-links">
    <?php print render($action_links); ?></ul><?php endif; ?>
    <?php print render($page['content']); ?>
    <?php print $feed_icons; ?>
  </div></div> <!-- /.section, #content -->

  <?php if ($page['sidebar_first']): ?>
    <div id="sidebar-first" class="column sidebar">
    <div class="section">
      <?php print render($page['sidebar_first']); ?>
    </div></div> <!-- /.section, #sidebar-first -->
  <?php endif; ?>

  <?php if ($page['sidebar_second']): ?>
    <div id="sidebar-second" class="column sidebar">
    <div class="section">
      <?php print render($page['sidebar_second']); ?>
    </div></div> <!-- /.section, #sidebar-second -->
```

```
        <?php endif; ?>
    </div></div> <!-- /#main, /#main-wrapper →
```

An important thing to notice in the code above is that the content of the page is rendered as a block within the `$page['content']` variable. This makes it very easy to reposition the main site content anywhere on screen.

The template ends by displaying the footer section:

```
    <div id="footer"><div class="section">
      <?php print theme('links', array('links' => $secondary_menu,
      'attributes' => array('id' => 'secondary-menu',
      'class' => array('links', 'clearfix')),
      'heading' => t('Secondary menu'))); ?>
      <?php print render($page['footer']); ?>
    </div></div> <!-- /.section, /#footer -->
```

This section has again been simplified by removing the Drupal 6 `$footer_message` variable and simply adding this information to the footer region of the page.

There are a number of ways to override the `page.tpl.php` template in your custom theme. All of the methods available in Drupal 6 are still available. You can still use the following formats:

- page.tpl.php
- page-*content-type*.tpl.php
- page-*content-type-node-id*.tpl.php

Drupal 7 also adds a fourth type of override. In Drupal 7, you can name a template file page-*content-type*-%.tpl.php, which allows you to use the template for only instances of the content type without changing the behavior of edit forms or other views within the content-type.

Theming individual regions with region.tpl.php

The `region.tpl.php` template was added to eliminate redundant code that was used in the `page.tpl.php` template. The actual content of the template is very simple:

```
<?php
// $Id: region.tpl.php,v 1.1 2009/10/05 02:43:01 webchick Exp $
/**
 * @file
```

```
 * Default theme implementation to display a region.
 *
 * Available variables:
 * - $content: The content for this region, typically blocks.
 * - $classes: String of classes that can be used to style
contextually through CSS. It can be manipulated through the variable
$classes_array from preprocess functions. The default values can be
one or more of the following:
 *    - region: The current template type, i.e., "theming hook".
 *    - region-[name]: The name of the region with underscores replaced
with dashes. For example, the page_top region would have a region-
page-top class.
 * - $region: The name of the region variable as defined in the
theme's .info file.
 *
 * Helper variables:
 * - $classes_array: Array of html class attribute values. It is
flattened
 *    into a string within the variable $classes.
 * - $is_admin: Flags true when the current user is an administrator.
 * - $is_front: Flags true when presented in the front page.
 * - $logged_in: Flags true when the current user is a logged-in
member.
 *
 * @see template_preprocess()
 * @see template_preprocess_region()
 * @see template_process()
 */
?>
<div class="<?php print $classes; ?>">
  <?php print $content; ?>
</div>
```

The code merely wraps the content of the region with a div that has classes based on the region being rendered. Most themes will not need to override this template. However, you can use this template to render specific regions different from your normal regions.

Theming individual nodes with node.tpl.php

The other template that you will most likely override in your theme is the `node.tpl.php` template, which renders the content of nodes. This file has also changed in Drupal 7. Let's look at the full file before we investigate each section in detail:

```php
<?php
// $Id: node.tpl.php,v 1.29 2009/12/06 01:00:27 dries Exp $
/**
 * @file
 * Default theme implementation to display a node.
 *
 * Available variables:
 * - $title: the (sanitized) title of the node.
 * - $content: An array of node items. Use render($content) to print
 * them all, or print a subset such as render($content['field_example']).
 * Use hide($content['field_example']) to temporarily suppress the
 * printing of a given element.
 * - $user_picture: The node author's picture from user-picture.tpl.
 * php.
 * - $date: Formatted creation date. Preprocess functions can reformat
 * it by calling format_date() with the desired parameters on the
 * $created variable.
 * - $name: Themed username of node author output from theme_
 * username().
 * - $node_url: Direct url of the current node.
 * - $terms: the themed list of taxonomy term links output from theme_
 * links().
 * - $display_submitted: whether submission information should be
 * displayed.
 * - $contextual_links (array): An array of contextual links for the
 * node.
 * - $classes: String of classes that can be used to style
 * contextually through CSS. It can be manipulated through the variable
 * $classes_array from preprocess functions. The default values can be
 * one or more of the following:
 *    - node: The current template type, i.e., "theming hook".
 *    - node-[type]: The current node type. For example, if the node is
 * a "Blog entry" it would result in "node-blog". Note that the machine
 * name will often be in a short form of the human readable label.
 *    - node-teaser: Nodes in teaser form.
 *    - node-preview: Nodes in preview mode.
 *    The following are controlled through the node publishing options.
 *    - node-promoted: Nodes promoted to the front page.
 *    - node-sticky: Nodes ordered above other non-sticky nodes in
 * teaser listings.
```

```
 *    - node-unpublished: Unpublished nodes visible only to
administrators.
 *
 * Other variables:
 * - $node: Full node object. Contains data that may not be safe.
 * - $type: Node type, i.e. story, page, blog, etc.
 * - $comment_count: Number of comments attached to the node.
 * - $uid: User ID of the node author.
 * - $created: Time the node was published formatted in Unix
timestamp.
 * - $classes_array: Array of html class attribute values. It is
flattened into a string within the variable $classes.
 * - $zebra: Outputs either „even" or „odd". Useful for zebra striping
in teaser listings.
 * - $id: Position of the node. Increments each time it's output.
 *
 * Node status variables:
 * - $build_mode: Build mode, e.g. ‚full', ‚teaser'...
 * - $teaser: Flag for the teaser state (shortcut for
 *   $build_mode == ‚teaser').
 * - $page: Flag for the full page state.
 * - $promote: Flag for front page promotion state.
 * - $sticky: Flags for sticky post setting.
 * - $status: Flag for published status.
 * - $comment: State of comment settings for the node.
 * - $readmore: Flags true if the teaser content of the node cannot
hold the main body content.
 * - $is_front: Flags true when presented in the front page.
 * - $logged_in: Flags true when the current user is a logged-in
member.
 * - $is_admin: Flags true when the current user is an administrator.
 * Field variables: for each field instance attached to the node a
corresponding variable is defined, e.g. $node->body becomes $body.
When needing to access a field's raw values, developers/themers are
strongly encouraged to use these variables. Otherwise they will
have to explicitly specify the desired field language, e.g. $node-
>body[‚en'], thus overriding any language negotiation rule that was
previously applied.
 *
 * @see template_preprocess()
 * @see template_preprocess_node()
 * @see template_process()
 */
?>
```

```php
<div id="node-<?php print $node->nid; ?>"
class="<?php print $classes; ?> clearfix"<?php print $attributes; ?>>

  <?php print $user_picture; ?>

  <?php if (!$page && !empty($contextual_links)): ?>
    <?php print render($contextual_links); ?>
  <?php endif; ?>

  <?php if (!$page): ?>
    <h2<?php print $title_attributes; ?>>
    <a href="<?php print $node_url; ?>"><?php print $node_title; ?>
    </a></h2>
  <?php endif; ?>

    <?php if ($display_submitted || !empty($content[,links'][,terms'])):
?>
    <div class="meta">
      <?php if ($display_submitted): ?>
        <span class="submitted">
          <?php
            print t(,Submitted by !username on !datetime',
              array(,!username' => $name, ,!datetime' => $date));
          ?>
        </span>
      <?php endif; ?>

      <?php if (!empty($content[,links'][,terms'])): ?>
        <div class="terms terms-inline"><?php print
        render($content[,links'][,terms']); ?></div>
      <?php endif; ?>
    </div>
  <?php endif; ?>

  <div class="content"<?php print $content_attributes; ?>>
    <?php
      // We hide the comments and links now so that we can render them
later.
      hide($content[,comments']);
      hide($content[,links']);
      print render($content);
    ?>
  </div>

  <?php print render($content[,links']); ?>

  <?php print render($content[,comments']); ?>
</div>
```

As with all of the templates we have looked at so far, the template starts with an explanation of the variables that are available within the template. Let's start by looking at the variables that have changed, been added, or been removed:

- The `$context` variable no longer contains a textual representation of the node. Instead, it now is an array of items that make up the node. This array can either be rendered completely using `render($content)`, or specific pieces of content can be rendered by calling `render($content['element_to_render'])`. If you are rendering the entire array at one time, you can prevent specific elements from being rendered by calling `hide($content['element_to_hide'])`.

- The author's picture has been renamed from `$picture` to `$author_picture`. You can now alter the appearance of the picture using the `user-picture.tpl.php` template.

- The `links` variable has now been moved within the `$content` array.

- Information about who the node was submitted by is no longer pre-themed and stored in the `$submitted` variable. Instead, the `$display_submitted` variable is passed. The submission information should only be displayed if this variable is set to true. Information from the `$name` and `$date` variables can be used to build the submission information.

- Contextual links are now returned, which represent links to other actions or content that are dependent on the current view.

- A `$classes` string, which is built from the `$classes_array` variable is now passed in. The `$classes_array` variable can be modified as needed during the preprocess hooks for the template including `theme_preprocess` and `theme_preprocess_node`. By default, classes are generated indicating the template type, node type, whether or not the node is a teaser or preview image, if the node is promoted to the front page, if the node is sticky, and if the node is unpublished. Additional classes may be added by other modules, or by themes.

- A `$build_mode` flag has been added to make it easier to understand what types of information the user desires. When you create custom templates, you should use this variable rather than the `$teaser` flag.

- Drupal will also pass a variable for each field of the node using the internal name of the field. Therefore, the body field becomes `$body` and a field named image would become `$image`. The formatted information for each field is also stored in the `$content` array, so you should only need to access these variables if you need to access the raw content. However, if you do need the raw content, you should use these variables as it will have information about the correct language already in it.

After the comment section, the template opens the div containing the node and prints any classes and attributes that have been defined for the node:

```
<div id="node-<?php print $node->nid; ?>"
class="<?php print $classes; ?> clearfix"<?php print $attributes; ?>>
```

This procedure is similar to the Drupal 6 procedure except that the the `$classes` variable is used rather than having the template attempt to determine the appropriate classes to display. Drupal 6 also used a clear-block class rather than the new clearfix class.

Next, the author's picture is displayed if it is set and any contextual links that were passed in are rendered:

```
<?php print $user_picture; ?>

<?php if (!$page && !empty($contextual_links)): ?>
  <?php print render($contextual_links); ?>
<?php endif; ?>
```

Since the `$user_picture` variable has already been rendered in a template, it is simply printed. The contextual links are new to Drupal 7. They are rendered after checking to ensure that they exist and should be printed.

The template now prints the title of the page:

```
<?php if (!$page): ?>
    <h2<?php print $title_attributes; ?>>
      <a href="<?php print $node_url; ?>">
        <?php print $node_title; ?>
      </a>
    </h2>
<?php endif; ?>
```

Again, this code is very similar to the Drupal 6 code. The only real addition is the rendering of the `$title_attributes` variable, which allows you to add additional classes to the node title or add any other HTML attributes you might want.

The next section of the template displays submission information if enabled, as well as taxonomy terms. These are both wrapped within a meta div, which the default Drupal 7 template ensures is not displayed when it is empty:

```
<?php if ($display_submitted || !empty($content['links']['terms'])):
?>
    <div class="meta">
      <?php if ($display_submitted): ?>
        <span class="submitted">
          <?php
```

```
            print t('Submitted by !username on !datetime',
              array('!username' => $name, '!datetime' => $date));
          ?>
        </span>
      <?php endif; ?>

      <?php if (!empty($content['links']['terms'])): ?>
        <div class="terms terms-inline">
        <?php print render($content['links']['terms']); ?></div>
      <?php endif; ?>
    </div>
  <?php endif; ?>
```

As mentioned earlier, the submission information is no longer passed to the node template pre-rendered. Therefore, it is rendered directly in this template. Similarly, the links are passed into the template through the `$content` array and are rendered within the template.

With the meta information displayed, the template is now ready to display the content, which it does using the following lines:

```
<div class="content"<?php print $content_attributes; ?>>
  <?php
    // We hide the comments and links now so that we can render them
      later.
    hide($content['comments']);
    hide($content['links']);
    print render($content);
  ?>
</div>
```

This code demonstrates the use of hiding specific sections within the `$content` array before rendering the entire `$content` array. In this case, the comments and links are removed and all remaining content is rendered. This allows the remaining content to be rendered in a specific order and wrapped within different div instances. The content that was excluded is now rendered by the template using the following code:

```
<?php print render($content['links']); ?>

<?php print render($content['comments']); ?>
```

This is similar to how the content was rendered within Drupal 6 except that comments were rendered with the main content.

At this point, the template closes the main div for the node and ends.

template.php

The `template.php` file is where you will override theme hooks to modify how information is displayed on your site. The basic functionality of this file is identical to the Drupal 6 version. However, a number of the hooks that you can implement have changed. We will explore all of the hooks in more detail shortly.

The other key change to the `template.php` file is that hook implementations must be prefixed with the name of the theme. They can no longer be prefixed with the theme engine name since this caused several problems with sub-themes including the possibility that a hook would be called multiple times.

Other changes

There are a few other changes to the template system that are worth mentioning:

- The only other major change to the theme templates is the removal of the `box.tpl.php` file. The `box.tpl.php` file was rarely used and the areas that did use them now have specific theme functions that can be used to control the display.

- The `block.tpl.php` template file has been moved from the system module to the block module for better consistency.

- As has been mentioned before, a number of special elements have been removed and replaced with blocks to simplify Drupal and make theming easier. The special content that has been removed includes: help, mission statement, content, and footer message.

New JavaScript functionality

Starting in Drupal 7, additional JavaScript tools have been included to make development easier and allow you to make your sites more dynamic. This also makes Drupal itself more dynamic and allows Drupal core to implement modern new functionality expected in today's websites.

jQuery tools

The following jQuery libraries are now included with Drupal by default:

- jQuery 1.3.2 — the latest version of jQuery is included with Drupal core and it is included on all pages by default so you don't need to do anything special to use jQuery in your theme.

- jQuery UI 1.7.2 — the latest version is included with Drupal in the `misc/ui` folder of the installation. Only UI core is included on all pages by default. If you want to utilize other scripts on your page, you will need to make appropriate calls to `drupal_add_js` and `drupal_add_css` from your theme or module.

- jQuery Forms 2.21 — jQuery Forms allow forms to utilize AJAX to submit the form. This functionality must be included with a call to `drupal_add_js` if you want to utilize it on a specific page.

- jQuery Once 1.2 — this plug-in allows you to ensure that a behavior only executes once. This reduces the amount of code needed to handle common jQuery tasks.

jQuery is a really easy library to work with in JavaScript and makes even complex tasks easy (or at least relatively easy). A full discussion of jQuery is beyond the scope of this book. For more information about jQuery, pick up either *Drupal 6 JavaScript and jQuery* or *Learning jQuery, 1.3* both from Packt Publishing.

AJAX framework from CTools

In addition to the new jQuery tools in Drupal 7, the AJAX framework from the popular CTools project maintained by merlinofchaos has been added to Drupal core. This new framework extends and may eventually replace the AHAH framework, which was introduced in Drupal 6.

The new AJAX framework allows you to define a custom callback that will handle the AJAX request and return information to the browser.

Additional information about this new framework is available at `http://drupal.org/node/544418`.

Including other JavaScript libraries

If none of these new libraries suit your needs or if it is not included by default, you can use the `drupal_add_js` method to include additional JavaScript files in your page. The signature of this method has changed from Drupal 6 to Drupal 7 and there are some new features available. The new method signature is:

```
drupal_add_js($data = NULL, $options = NULL)
```

The parameters that were added individually after the `$data` option are now included within the `$options` array.

You can now use `drupal_add_js` to add external files to the page. This is done by setting the type to external in the options array. For example, you can specify:

```
drupal_add_js('http://example.com/example.js', array('type' =>
'external');
```

CSS changes

Several changes have been made to the classes and IDs, which are available for styling your pages. These changes allow more granular control when styling your pages. Let's look into each change in detail.

System classes

Drupal 7 has modified the classes that are generated when the core blocks are used in your site. The new names are designed to make your CSS files easier to understand and make it easier for new themers to quickly style the built in blocks.

The following list contains the old and new IDs for each block:

Block Name	Drupal 6 ID	Drupal 7 ID
Recent blog posts	block-blog-0	block-blog-recent
Book navigation	block-book-0	block-book-navigation
Recent comments	block-comment-0	block-comment-recent
Active forum topics	block-forum-0	block-forum-active
New forum topics	block-forum-0	block-forum-new
Language Switcher	block-locale-0	block-locale-language-switcher
Syndicate	block-node-0	block-node-syndicate
Most recent poll	block-poll-0	block-poll-recent
Author information	block-profile-0	block-profile-author-information

Block Name	Drupal 6 ID	Drupal 7 ID
Search form	block-search-0	block-search-form
Popular content	block-statistics-0	block-statistics-popular
Powered by Drupal	block-system-0	block-system-powered-by
User Login	block-user-0	block-user-login
Navigation	block-user-1	block-user-navigation
Who's new	block-user-2	block-user-new
Who's online	block-user-3	block-user-online

To preserve the styling of these blocks in Drupal 7, you will need to modify your CSS file or files to refer to these elements using their new IDs. For example, this code in Drupal 6:

```
/* Add a blue border around the author information block */
#block-profile-0{
    border: 2px solid blue;
}
```

will look like the following in Drupal 7:

```
/* Add a blue border around the author information block */
#block-profile-author-information{
    border: 2px solid blue;
}
```

Classes array

As we saw earlier when we went through the node template, the classes for a node are now built in the `$classes_array` variable during the preprocess routines for a node. The classes to be applied are then flattened and can be easily rendered within the node template. If you were generating custom classes in your Drupal 6 theme, you should consider moving the generation to a preprocess routine in your Drupal 7 theme.

Hiding information

Drupal 7 has added several classes to make it easier to hide content generated by Drupal and to make hidden content more friendly to screen readers. These include:

- .element-hidden, which renders the content as completely invisible to all users including screen readers. This can be used to toggle collapsible fieldsets and other content that is only displayed when the user clicks on a specific link.

- .element-invisible, which makes the content invisible to normal users, but visible to screen readers. This allows you to easily provide alternate content for images, Flash videos, and other content that might be otherwise lost to visually impaired visitors. You should make sure to not include any links or other navigation elements within this content to avoid causing problems for visitors.

Theme API changes

Now that we have gone through the changes in the major Drupal templates and covered the major changes related to JavaScript and CSS, let's look into the changes to the actual theme API. These functions are implemented within your theme's template.php file and give you immense control over the presentation of elements within your site.

Signature changes

The first thing you will notice when you try to upgrade your Drupal 6 theme to Drupal 7 is that all functions now take a $variables array rather than a list of parameters in the method signature. This allows for consistent pre-processing of variables and makes coding easier. Unless noted otherwise later in this chapter, all parameters that used to be passed to a theme function are now available within the variables array using the original parameter name. For example, in Drupal 6, the theme_date method was implemented as follows:

```
function theme_date($element) {
  return theme('form_element', $element,
    '<div class="container-inline">' .
    $element['#children'] .
    '</div>');
}
```

In Drupal 7, the same function is implemented as:

```
function theme_date($variables) {
  $element = $variables['element'];
  return '<div class="container-inline">' .
    drupal_render_children($element) .
    '</div>');
}
```

To override a theme hook in your custom theme, you will need to replace the word theme in the function name with the name of the theme. So for the drupal_7_rocks theme to override the `theme_date` hook, it would create a function called `drupal_7_rocks_date` in the `template.php` file.

Alter hooks

In Drupal 6, themers were unable to use the `hook_alter` functions like `hook_form_alter`, `hook_page_alter`, `hook_js_alter`, and `hoook_css_alter`. This resulted in many production themes needing to implement a module that only implemented these methods for the theme. Managing the module in addition to the theme was a hassle that caused lots of extra work for production site administrators. Thankfully, in Drupal 7, this restriction has been lifted and themes can now implement these functions. Care should be taken to ensure that only presentation-related changes are made within the theme. If you need to change functionality, you should implement a module instead.

As always, these are implemented by replacing the word hook with the internal name of your theme. For example, to implement `hook_css_alter` for the theme drupal_7_rocks, you would use the function:

```
/**
 * Implement hook_css_alter().
 */
function drupal_7_rocks_css_alter(&$css) {
  //Remove unwanted css files and/or
  //add additional theme specific css.
}
```

New methods

Let's look at the new theme hooks that are available within Drupal 7. In this book, we will limit our discussion to a listing of the method as well a description of what the method does. If you need more information including information about the default implementation, visit `http://api.drupal.org` and enter the name of the function you want more information on.

template_preprocess_menu_tree(&$variables)

This method allows you to add additional information about menu items to the menu tree including adding classes to different levels within the tree. This method is called before any rendering is done.

template_preprocess_username(&$variables)

Allows you to alter information related to the name of the active user as well as links to the user's profile and home page. This method is called before any rendering is done.

template_process_username(&$variables)

Provides a second level of processing to the username, which is completed after all modules have had a chance to preprocess the data.

theme_admin_block($variables)

Allows you to override the display of blocks for site administrators. You can display the title, description, and content of the block.

theme_confirm_form($variables)

Allows you to change how confirmation forms are displayed. By default, no changes are made to the default rendering of forms. However, you can add additional text or classes to the form.

theme_container($variables)

Displays a container for related items within a form.

theme_dashboard($variables)

Controls the appearance of the dashboard within the administrative interface. The default implementation also uses this method to add the CSS file controlling the overall appearance of the dashboard.

theme_dashboard_admin($variables)

Displays the area of the dashboard that allows you to customize the dashboard. This is a full list of available blocks that can be added to the dashboard.

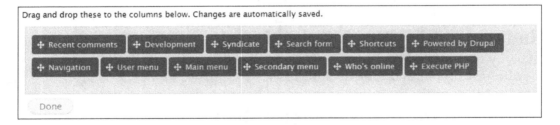

theme_dashboard_disabled_block($variables)

Displays a single block, which is disabled in the dashboard. Only used while the user is customizing the dashboard.

theme_dashboard_disabled_blocks($variables)

Themes a group of disabled blocks in the dashboard. Only used while the user is customizing the dashboard.

theme_dashboard_region($variables)

Themes a region within the dashboard. By default, the dashboard has a main region and a sidebar region.

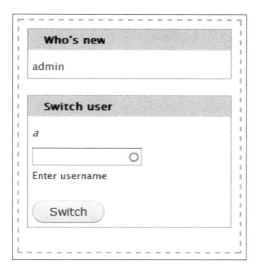

theme_filter_guidelines($variables)

Renders the guidelines for a Text format within a content creation page. The guidelines describe how the Text format behaves.

theme_form_element_label($variables)

Displays a label for a field within a form. If the field is required, a required marker is output. The actual marker is rendered using the `theme_form_required_marker` function which is coming up next.

theme_form_required_marker($variables)

Displays the indicator that a field is required. In the previous screenshot, the required marker is the red asterisk.

theme_forum_form($variables)

Another convenience function similar to the `confirm_form` hook. This allows you to override the display of just the form to create forums.

theme_html_tag($variables)

Controls the display of an HTML tag, which appears within the head section of a document. The default implementation can render additional attributes and prefixes and suffixes to allow the rendering of CDATA content.

theme_image_anchor($variables)

Displays a group of radio boxes that are used to control the anchor point when an image is processed.

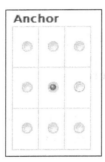

theme_image_crop_summary($variables)

Displays a summary of the settings for a crop operation when image styles are being created.

theme_image_resize_summary($variables)

Displays a summary of the settings for a resize operation when image styles are being created.

theme_image_rotate_summary($variables)

Displays a summary of the settings for a rotation operation when image styles are being created.

theme_image_scale_summary($variables)

Displays a summary of the settings for a scale operation when image styles are being created.

theme_image_style_effects($variables)

Displays a list of all image effects that have been added to a style and allows users to add, remove, or reorder the effects in a style.

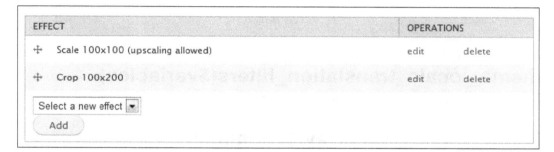

theme_image_style_list($variables)

Displays a list of all image styles that are available within the system, with all operations that can be taken on each style.

theme_image_style_preview($variables)

Creates and displays a preview of the effects of applying an image style to an example image.

theme_link($variables)

Called from the l() function. This method allows you to override the rendering of links in the system. Before overriding this method, you should carefully consider if there is another method of accomplishing your end goal because using the theme_link hook can slow down the rendering of your site considerably.

theme_locale_date_format_form($variables)

Themes the form to control the date formats that are selected for a
particular language.

theme_locale_languages_configure_form($variables)

Renders the form, which allows you to configure the languages that are available
on the site and adds additional information for proper configuration.

	ENGLISH NAME	NATIVE NAME	CODE	DIRECTION	ENABLED	DEFAULT	OPERATIONS
✛	**English**	English	en	Left to right	☑	⦿	edit
✛	**Spanish**	Español	es	Left to right	☑	◯	edit delete

theme_locale_translation_filters($variables)

Gives you control over the locale translation form generated by the locale module.

theme_menu_link(array $variables)

Generates the HTML for a specific link within a menu. This gives you a lot of control
over how the menu appears.

theme_menu_local_action($variables)

Generates the HTML for a local action within a node.

theme_rdf_metadata($variables)

This function generates RDFa content as a series of empty spans containing attributes
describing the content that is understood by RDFa parsers.

theme_rdf_template_variable_wrapper($variables)

Generates a wrapper around an HTML element that contains additional RDF information about the element. This method is only needed for template variables that need containing attributes. If you are already outputting the proper attributes in your templates, you can override this method to not wrap the variable by calling:

```
drupal_attributes($rdf_template_variable_attributes_array[$variable_
name]);
```

theme_shortcut_set_customize($variables)

Renders the list of shortcuts that exist within a set of shortcuts and properly handles rearranging existing shortcuts and properly displaying shortcuts that have not been set.

Using set "Default" (Change set)		
NAME	OPERATIONS	
Enabled		
✛ Add content	edit	delete
✛ Find content	edit	delete
✛ Dashboard	edit	delete
Empty		
Empty		
Empty		
Empty		
Disabled		

theme_system_compact_link()

Renders a link to show or hide inline help descriptions.

theme_system_date_time_settings($variables)

Generates the display for the date settings form:

DATE TYPE	FORMAT		OPERATIONS
Long	Saturday, December 12, 2009 - 21:58 ▾		
Medium	Sat, 12/12/2009 - 21:58 ▾		
Short	12/12/2009 - 21:58 ▾		
Extra Long	Saturday, December 12, 2009 - 9:58pm ▾		delete

theme_system_modules_fieldset($variables)

Used to display the list of modules that are available on the site with information about the modules that it requires and the modules that require it to be activated so that administrators can enable modules.

theme_system_modules_incompatible($variables)

Properly renders a message to indicate an incompatibility.

theme_system_run_cron_image($variables)

Generates content to run cron if a user's browser does not support JavaScript. You should not override this hook unless you have a strong understanding of the cron system.

theme_system_settings_form($variables)

Like some of the other hooks we have seen, this is provided as a convenience if you need to override the settings form.

theme_system_themes_page($variables)

Generates the content for the page, which allows administrators to select the theme for the site and enable new themes.

theme_text_format_wrapper($variables)

This method is in charge of properly wrapping a form element that can utilize text formats.

theme_update_last_check($variables)

Displays information about when Drupal last checked for updates to Drupal and any installed modules and themes. The method also adds a link to check for updates manually.

theme_update_manager_update_form($variables)

Themes the form that allows a site administrator to select which projects should be updated as well as which version each project should be updated to.

theme_user_admin_permissions($variables)

Controls the display of the permissions page to allow site administrators to control what actions each user can take within the site.

theme_vertical_tabs($variables)

Renders fieldsets for an element as the new vertical tabs element. We saw this element extensively when creating content, content types, and so on.

Removed methods

Now that we have looked into the methods that Drupal 7 has added for themers, let's take a quick look at the methods that were removed. We will also look at some potential ways of replacing the functions that were removed:

Method Name	Additional Information
theme_blocks	This was only used by the chameleon theme, which is no longer included in core.
theme_box	This function was only used in the comment module and search form and the functionality is now directly implemented.
theme_closure	This hook was removed since closure is now handled with $page_bottom variable, which is rendered in html.tpl.php.

Method Name	Additional Information
theme_comment_admin_overview	These hooks were all removed after comments were simplified in Drupal 7.
theme_comment_controls	
theme_comment_flat_collapsed	
theme_comment_flat_expanded	
theme_comment_submitted	
theme_comment_thread_collapsed	
theme_comment_thread_expanded	
theme_comment_view	
theme_help	Removed in favor of having help be a block rather than a special piece of content.
theme_item	This hook was no longer needed due to changes to the code that called it and was removed.
theme_menu_item	These methods are no longer needed due to the ability to add classes to an element and preprocess variables.
theme_menu_item_link	This is not needed due to the ability to add localized options to any link element.
theme_node_admin_nodes	This is no longer needed due to changes in the form.
theme_node_submitted	This was removed in favor of direct theming within the node.tpl.php template.
theme_password_confirm	This is no longer needed due to the new password validation functionality.
theme_system_modules	This hook was replaced with theme_system_module_fieldset.
theme_system_themes_form	These hooks were replaced with theme_system_themes_page.
theme_system_theme_select_form	
theme_taxonomy_term_page	This is no longer needed due to changes in the form.

Method Name	Additional Information
`theme_taxonomy_term_ select`	This is no longer needed because the taxonomy term is a simple select box that can be rendered using the normal theme system.
`theme_token`	This function just marked elements as hidden. There are now better ways of handling this in Drupal 7.
`theme_upload_ attachments`	These hooks were changed due to the removal of the upload module in favor of file fields.
`theme_upload_form_ current`	
`theme_upload_form_ new`	
`theme_user_admin_ account`	These hooks were not called in Drupal 6. Therefore, they were removed in Drupal 7.
`theme_user_admin_ perm`	
`theme_xml_icon`	This hook was replaced by `theme_feed_icon` in Drupal 6 and has been removed in Drupal 7.

Upgrading Drupal 6 themes to Drupal 7

The process of converting Drupal 6 themes to Drupal 7 involves modifying your theme to take advantage of all of the new features and modifying the syntax of your method calls to utilize the new method syntax. Any calls to functionality that has been removed will also need to be revised. You can find a complete list of changes that need to be made at: `http://drupal.org/update/theme/6/7`.

You can use the following basic procedure for updating your theme to Drupal 7:

1. Update your `.info` file to include any additional scripts and CSS files that are needed by your site and make sure to include `style.css` and `script.js` if you use them.

2. Modify the structure of your `page.tpl.php` page to remove the information contained in `html.tpl.php`.

3. Modify the rendering of each region to use `region.tpl.php` and to load content from the `$page` variable.

4. Replace removed special content types with blocks as needed.

5. Change variable names that have been modified including the `main_menu` and `secondary_menu`.

6. Add additional classes to HTML elements as needed to render the page.

7. Update `template.php` to utilize the new API method signatures.

8. Replace method calls that have been removed with new functionality.

9. Test everything and continue to tweak as needed.

Summary

In this chapter, we have gone through all of the major changes to the Drupal theme system that were introduced in Drupal 7. We looked at changes to the template files, changes for JavaScript, changes for CSS, API changes, and finally we worked through a basic roadmap for upgrading an existing Drupal 6 theme to Drupal 7.

Hopefully, you now have a solid understanding of the new features available to you in Drupal 7 and can take advantage of all of the new tools.

In the next chapter, we will be looking into the changes made to the Drupal API, which will affect module developers.

6

Drupal 7 Database Changes

In the last chapter, we looked at changes to the theming system that were introduced in Drupal 7. These changes have made the API more robust and easier to use. They also make it easier to implement high quality themes for your site.

In this chapter, we will look at changes to the database abstraction layer of the Drupal API. There are several significant changes to the Drupal API that have been made for version 7. The biggest of these is the new DBTNG layer, which provides an abstracted layer between Drupal and the database that stores your content. We will explore the DBTNG layer in detail during this chapter. In the next chapter, we will explore the other major changes and new features of the API including:

- Using the Field API
- Image handling API
- Revised tokens and actions
- RDF API
- Permissions changes
- Taxonomy changes and much more...

Without further ADO, let's start looking into the new DBTNG layer, which is critical for all Drupal 7 modules.

What is DBTNG?

DBTNG is the new database abstraction layer that makes connecting to and querying the database much easier in Drupal 7 than it was in the previous version of Drupal. DBTNG is an acronym for Database Layer: The Next Generation.

Background

DBTNG was built with the intention of making it easier to support additional types of databases. Prior to Drupal 7, it was theoretically possible to create a Drupal-compliant compatibility layer to support any database. However, this required quite a lot of custom code and each custom module typically needed to add customized SQL statements to support multiple databases. In practice, this meant that Drupal only fully supported MySQL and PostgreSQL. Most contributed modules only supported MySQL although some also supported PostgreSQL. Site administrators who wanted to use a different database needed to do a great deal of work to migrate modules or build their own modules with support for their database of choice.

Some of the other key goals for DBTNG were:

- Support for multiple database servers
- Provide support for transactions
- Provide an interface to make building complex dynamic queries easier
- Ensure that security checks are enforced and cannot be overridden
- Make it easier for custom modules to intercept and enhance queries generated in core or in other custom modules

The new DBTNG layer is based on the PHP PDO (PHP Data Objects) library. The PDO library is designed to give developers a consistent interface to access any database that has a PDO-compatible driver from PHP. The PDO interface is completely object-oriented, which means that DBTNG also uses object-oriented constructs to deliver its functionality.

Key concepts in DBTNG

There are several key concepts that you need to be aware of when working with DBTNG. Many of these concepts are derived from PDO so if you are familiar with that, you will have no problem transitioning to DBTNG.

Drivers

Drivers in DBTNG are in charge of taking the base statement built by the user and transforming it into a SQL statement that is valid for the database you are working with. Each database type must have a driver built for it to work with Drupal 7. The default installation includes drivers for MySQL, PostgreSQL, and SQLite. Other drivers may be available after release as custom modules or patches.

Drivers are installed in the `includes/database` directory of your Drupal installation. Each driver is given its own sub-folder, which should be named based on the database name and it should typically only contain lower case letters.

Drivers typically consist of four include files that contain classes which override core database functionality. These include:

- `database.inc` — contains classes related to database connection as well as providing the possibility to override functionality needed by DBTNG that is not provided by the database, and to optimize DBTNG functionality, which has a direct implementation within the database.

- `install.inc` — contains a class to extend the core `DatabaseTasks` class with functionality that is needed to prepare a database for use with Drupal.

- `query.inc` — contains classes which override the core classes that implement the core query classes including `InsertQuery`, `UpdateQuery`, `SelectQuery`, `MergeQuery`, `DeleteQuery`, and `TruncateQuery`.

- `schema.inc` — contains classes to define how the driver should create tables and columns within the database as well as return information about the structure of the database.

A complete description of building new database drivers is beyond the scope of this book. However, additional information is available at: `http://drupal.org/node/310087`.

Connections

Connections are extended from PDO connections (the PDO class). Each database that is configured within the Drupal `settings.php` file is given a single Database connection object that is active throughout the page request. In general, you should not need to work with the connection object directly unless you are doing a very complex database manipulation involving multiple databases.

You can retrieve the currently active connection within your module using the following statement:

```php
<?php
$conn = Database::getConnection();
?>
```

You can modify the active connection using the following statement:

```php
<?php
db_set_active($key);
?>
```

Where `$key` is the key of the database in the `$databases` array within `settings.php`. All sites will have the default key defined. And, in most cases, this is the only database defined.

The following snippet taken directly from `settings.php` shows the location of the key name and target name within the `settings.php` file:

```php
$databases = array (
  'keyname' =>
  array (
    'targetname' =>
    array (
      'driver' => 'mysql',
      'database' => 'databasename',
      'username' => 'username',
      'password' => 'password',
      'host' => 'localhost',
      'port' => '',
    ),
  ),
);
```

If you need to manually open a connection you can do so by specifying the target and key of the connection to be opened as shown in the next code snippet:

```php
<?php
$conn = Database::getConnection($target, $key);
?>
```

A new connection will only be opened the first time that a request for it is made. This prevents unnecessary connections from being made and not used for each page load.

You can define connections to additional databases by adding information about them to your `settings.php` file. For example, to define a connection to a secondary SQLite database, you would add information about it after the default Drupal database has been defined as shown in the following snippet:

```php
<?php
$databases['default']['default'] = array(
  'driver' => 'mysql',
```

```
  'database' => 'drupaldb1',
  'username' => 'username',
  'password' => 'secret',
  'host' => 'dbserver1',
);
$databases['extra']['default'] = array(
  'driver' => 'sqlite',
  'file' => 'files/extradb.sqlite',
);
?>
```

In this case, the secondary database would be accessed using the `extra` key.

Statements

Statements are used to retrieve data from the database. This information can then be displayed on the page or used within calculations. A DBTNG statement represents a `SELECT` statement in SQL and is of type `DatabaseStatement` (unless the `DatabaseStatement` class has been sub-classed within the database driver). The `DatabaseStatement` is derived from the `PDOStatement` class within PDO.

When a statement is executed against a connection, the DBTNG layer will perform the following operations:

1. Build a prepared statement using PDO.
2. Set up the parameters for the statement using data passed to the query.
3. Execute the prepared statement.
4. Return the result set to the user.

The key difference between Drupal `DatabaseStatement` and the `PDOStatement` is that Drupal does not expose the prepared statement to the developer. This ensures that the prepared statement cannot be changed incorrectly and makes the module code significantly easier to read. We will look into statements in much more detail shortly.

Queries

Queries represent SQL statements that are sent to the database connections that manipulate data including inserts, deletes, updates, and so on. A query can either be created using a traditional SQL statement string or it can be built using the object-oriented query builder.

We will look at the various types of queries in more detail after we explore select statements in detail.

Using select statements

As discussed earlier, select statements allow you to retrieve information from the database. There are several methods of doing this in Drupal 7 depending on whether you want to use a procedural or object-oriented syntax and whether or not the SQL statement to be executed is provided by the developer or if the SQL statement is built by Drupal. Let's start by looking at queries where the statement is provided to Drupal.

Static queries

Static queries use SQL statements that are provided to the DBTNG layer rather than being built by Drupal. For example, to get a list of all nodes in the system, you can call:

```php
<?php
  $result = db_query("SELECT nid, title FROM {node}");
?>
```

This statement simply returns the node ID and title of all nodes within the system.

You may have noticed that the name of the table, in this case node, is surrounded by curly braces. Similar to Drupal 6, you can surround a table with curly braces which causes Drupal to automatically prefix the table based on the settings file. Table prefixing allows multiple sites to use the same database.

If you prefer a more object-oriented syntax, you can also make the same call using:

```php
<?php
$result = Database::getConnection()->query(
      "SELECT nid, title FROM {node}");
?>
```

Although this performs the same operations, the first statement is easier to read and therefore preferred.

Static queries using db_query are easy to write, and easy to read, but don't take full advantage of the DBTNG layer including several important security features. When you are migrating your modules to Drupal 7, consider replacing all static queries with dynamic queries even if it takes a little longer to do the conversion.

Limiting the data returned

If you need to limit the amount of data you want returned, you can use the `db_query_range` method which allows you to set both the starting record to retrieve as well as the number of records that should be retrieved. For example, if you want to get a list of all nodes in the database, 20 rows at a time starting at row 60, you would call:

```php
<?php
  $result = db_query_range(
      "SELECT nid, title FROM {node}", 60, 20);
?>
```

 If you want to paginate a query, consider using dynamic query objects that are extended with the `PagerDefault` extension.

Adding parameters to static queries

Most of the time when you are querying the database, you will need to pass additional information to the database to influence which rows are returned based on user input or the current page. For example, if you want to search nodes created after a specific date, you will want to use query parameters.

There are two ways in which parameters can be added to a query. You can either use an indexed arrays of parameters or you can use named parameters. Using named parameters is preferred though because it leads to much more readable code.

To add a named parameter, you simply insert the name you want into the query prefixed with a colon, and then provide an associative array as the `$args` parameter, where the key of the array is the name of the parameter. Let's look at some sample code:

```php
<?php
$result = db_query("SELECT nid, title FROM {node}
   WHERE created > :created",
   array(':created' => REQUEST_TIME - 3600,
)));
?>
```

In this example, the parameter is called `:created` and is set to the current time minus one hour.

Multiple parameters can be defined within a single database query so that you can query based on a number of different factors. You can even provide an array of values for a single parameter. This is mostly useful when you are using the IN operator within a query. In this example, the `:nids` parameters will be automatically expanded to include all elements from the array:

```php
<?php
// This code:
db_query("SELECT * FROM {node} WHERE nid IN (:nids)",
    array(':nids' => array(13, 42, 144));
?>
```

This will translate to:

```php
<?php
// This code:
db_query("SELECT * FROM {node} WHERE nid IN (13, 42, 144)",
?>
```

when the query is run.

If you prefer to use indexed arrays to supply parameters, simply replace the parameter name with a question mark and make sure to pass all parameters in the order they appear in the query. In this way, the first example query could be rewritten as:

```php
<?php
$result = db_query("SELECT nid, title FROM {node}
    WHERE created > ?",
    array(REQUEST_TIME - 3600,
));
?>
```

When in doubt, always use named parameters for your queries though.

Query options

The final parameter which can be supplied to the `db_query` and `db_query_range` methods is `$options`. This parameter allows you to control how the query is executed and how data is returned. There are several options that can be specified as described below:

* `target` — determines which target the query should be executed against if multiple targets exist within a connection. If the specified target cannot be used, the default target will be used.

- `fetch`—determines how data should be fetched from the result set. By default, the data for each row will be read into an object similar to using `db_fetch_object` in Drupal 6. The available methods of fetching data are defined by PDO and we will discuss them all in more detail when we get to the section on working with result sets.

- `return`—this option determines what information should be returned after the statement is executed. The default return type varies depending on the statement or query being executed. Options include:

   ◦ `Database::RETURN_STATEMENT`—returns the statement containing all results so you can iterate and process all results. This is the default for queries and select statements.

   ◦ `Database::RETURN_AFFECTED`—returns the number of rows that were affected by the query. This is the default for update and delete statements.

   ◦ `Database::RETURN_INSERT_ID`—returns the ID of the row which was just inserted. Used with Insert statements.

   ◦ `Database::RETURN_NULL`—returns nothing. Useful when there is no meaningful data to return.

- `throw_exception`—determines how exceptions are handled. This can be set to `TRUE` or `FALSE`. If it is set to `TRUE`, the default, any errors are logged and then rethrown so the calling code can handle it. If the option is set false, the error will be silently ignored.

Additional options may be available depending on the database driver you are using. To find a complete list of options that are available, check the `defaultOptions` method of your driver.

Saving query results to a temporary table

Drupal gives you the option to save the results of a query into a temporary table, which can improve performance for very complicated queries. The temporary table results are only available for the duration of the page request after which they are automatically deleted. The query will return the name of the temporary table that was created. This functionality is very similar to the Drupal 6 functionality of the same name; however, the method was changed to accept arguments and options similar to the `db_query` and `db_query_range` methods.

Dynamic queries

Although static queries are easy to build and use, at least for simple queries, the new dynamic query builder in Drupal 7 can be much easier to use and understand, especially with complex queries.

All dynamic queries begin with a call to db_select, which sets up a SelectQuery for the table and prepares the query for additional work.

The syntax for the db_select method is:

```
db_select($table, $alias = NULL, array $options = array())
```

The $table parameter should be the name of the main table you want to query. If you want to refer to the table using different names later, you can specify an $alias for the table. This is identical to using the as clause within an SQL statement. The options are identical to the options used in the db_query method.

Let's convert a basic query to select all information about all nodes into a dynamic query. The static query:

```php
<?php
  $result = db_query("SELECT * FROM {node} as n");
?>
```

will be transformed into the following dynamic query:

```php
<?php
  $query = db_select('node', 'n');
  $result = $query->execute();
?>
```

You will notice that the name of the table is not surrounded with curly braces. The DBTNG layer is smart enough to automatically prefix any table names that require prefixing.

After your query has been built, you will need to execute it using the execute method. The result of the execute method is a result set that is exactly the same as the result returned by the db_query method.

Working with fields

In the last example, we simply selected all of the data within the node table. However, this is very inefficient if you only care about a couple of columns within the table. To determine which columns will be returned in the query, we use the addField method of the query object.

The syntax of the `addField` method is:

```
addField($table_alias, $field, $alias = NULL)
```

Let's start by selecting just the node ID and title columns of the node table using the previous example as a basis:

```php
<?php
  $query = db_select('node', 'n');
  $query->addField('n', array('nid', 'title'));
  $result = $query->execute();
?>
```

As you can see, you can specify multiple fields in the same call by passing an array of fields to include as the `$field` parameter. This is a great way of quickly adding the fields you want. However, sometimes, you will also need to specify an alias for the field. This is especially important when you are querying multiple tables that have columns with the same name. In this case, you can provide an alias as the third parameter. However, you can only add one field at a time if you provide an alias. Let's modify the previous example to alias the title field as `node_title`:

```php
<?php
  $query = db_select('node', 'n');
  $query->addField('n', 'nid');
  $query->addField('n', 'title', 'node_title');
  $result = $query->execute();
?>
```

If you need to get a list of fields that have been added to a query, you can use the `getFields` method to retrieve the array of fields. The fields array is returned by reference so you can modify the individual fields if needed.

Ordering results

So far, we have allowed the database to determine what order the records are received in. However, you will often need to access the data in a particular order. You can do this using the `orderBy` and `orderRandom` methods. These have the following syntax:

```
orderBy($field, $direction = 'ASC')
orderRandom()
```

To use the `orderBy` method, you simply give it the name of a field to sort by and the direction you want to sort the records, either `ASC` for ascending sort or `DESC` for a descending sort. Let's modify our example to sort the table based on the creation date of the node:

```php
<?php
  $query = db_select('node', 'n');
  $query->addField('n', array('nid', 'title'));
  $query->orderBy('created', 'DESC');
  $result = $query->execute();
?>
```

The `orderRandom` method will randomize any records that have the same sort value. Therefore, if you first sort a set of nodes by author name and then randomize the records, it will return the records for each author in random order.

> If you want to give users the ability to sort data that is being displayed on your site, consider using the `TableSort` extender.

Joining tables

Up to now, we have only queried a single table at a time. Frequently, you will need to retrieve data from multiple tables. To do this, you use one of the `join` methods:

- `join` — adds a default join to the query. The actual default type of join is left up to the database driver.

- `innerJoin` — the tables on both the left and right side must have a row that matches the join condition for a record to be returned.

- `leftJoin` — the table on the left must have a row that matched the join condition, but the right side does not have to have a match. In other words, data on the right side can be null.

- `rightJoin` — the table on the right must have a row that matched the join condition, but the left side does not have to have a match. In other words, data on the left side can be null.

- `addJoin` — this is the function that typically does all of the work and the other 4 functions simply call this method.

The first four methods all have the same method signature:

```
join($table, $alias = NULL, $condition = NULL, $arguments = array())
```

The addJoin method is very similar; however, it takes an additional parameter as the first argument, which represents the type of join to be added:

```
addJoin($type, $table, $alias = NULL, $condition = NULL, $arguments =
array())
```

You can certainly call the addJoin method, but it is preferable to call one of the other four methods to improve readability. To use one of the join methods, you must specify the table you want to join. Next, you can optionally specify an alias for the table. This functions identically to the call to db_select and gives you the ability to define how the table will be referenced in other parts of the query. If you do not provide an alias, Drupal will automatically create one for you and return it from the function. Next, you should specify the condition used to join the two tables. If you do not specify a join condition, Drupal will attempt to find an appropriate method of joining the tables based on the fields in each table. However, it is much better to explicitly define the join conditions. Finally, you can specify any arguments that need to be added to the join criteria based on user input. Again, this functions identically to the arguments passed to the db_query method.

All of this may be a bit confusing so let's work through a practical example of joining the node table with the user table to get additional information about the author of a node:

```php
<?php
  $query = db_select('node', 'n');
  $query->addField('n', array('nid', 'title'));
  $query->orderBy('created', 'DESC');
  $table_alias = $query->join('users', 'u', 'n.uid = u.uid');
  $query->addField('u', 'name', 'author');
  $result = $query->execute();
?>
```

This will return a list of all nodes in the system with the name of the user who created the node labeled author.

Preventing duplicate records

When you start joining multiple tables together, it is possible to create situations where a record will be listed in the result set more than once. You can prevent this situation using the distinct method. This method will add the DISTINCT statement to the generated SQL statement, which will remove all duplicate records. There is a performance penalty to using distinct, so try to make sure that there isn't a better alternate method of removing duplicates from your query before resorting to this method.

Retrieving summary information

Many times, you are not as interested in the actual data within a table so much as a summary of information about the data. For example, you may want to get a count of the number of rows matching a particular query. This is easily done with the query object by calling the countQuery method. This method has the added benefit of reducing the query to a single row that has only a single field in it. We can retrieve the total number of nodes in the system with the following code:

```php
<?php
  $query = db_select('node', 'n');
  $num_rows = $query->countQuery()->execute()->fetchField();
?>
```

If you would like to retrieve other summary information, you can use grouping and expressions. The groupBy method tells Drupal how the query you are creating should be aggregated when building expressions. For example, you can group by the uid field of the node table to generate a count of nodes created by each author or you could group by a creation date to generate a count of nodes entered each day. To use the groupBy method, you simply specify the field that you want to group based on. You can call this function multiple times to group on multiple fields. Let's extend our running example to group our nodes based on the user who created the node:

```php
<?php
  $query = db_select('node', 'n');
  $query->addField('n', array('nid', 'title'));
  $table_alias = $query->join('users', 'u', 'n.uid = u.uid');
  $query->addField('u', 'uid', 'user_id');
  $query->addField('u', 'name', 'author');
  $query->groupBy('user_id');
  $result = $query->execute();
?>
```

The field name provided to the `groupBy` method should be the alias of a field or expression. You should either provide the alias when you add the field or use the alias returned from the `addField` or `addExpression` method.

Most of the time when you group data to generate summary information, you will use an expression to calculate additional information about the data. For example, you can COUNT the number of values, SUM the values to get a total, return the MAX value, or MIN value of a column, etc. The actual calculations that are available will vary depending on the underlying database so you should be careful to ensure that the SQL function you want to use is part of standard SQL and is widely supported if you want your module to be used by a wide audience. We look into expressions in more depth in the next section.

Using expressions to retrieve and manipulate data

As we discussed above, expressions allow you to manipulate data in the database to generate summary information, calculate derivative information, manipulate dates, and much more. Expressions are added to queries using the `addExpression` method, the complete signature of which is as follows:

```
addExpression($expression, $alias = NULL, $arguments = array())
```

This expression defines the SQL snippet that will be added to the query. The alias is used to refer to the result of the expression in other locations. If you do not provide an alias, Drupal will automatically build an alias for you named `expression_n` where n is a number to make the alias unique. The arguments variable is used to provide values for any parameters used in the expression.

A full discussion of all operators that are available for all databases is beyond the scope of this book. More information on the available operators for MySQL, PostgreSQL, and SQLite is available at the following locations:

- MySQL: `http://dev.mysql.com/doc/refman/5.5/en/functions.html`
- PostgreSQL: `http://www.postgresql.org/docs/8.4/interactive/functions.html`
- SQLite: `http://www.sqlite.org/lang.html`

Let's look at an example of using expressions using an operator that is available in all databases. If you create multiple revisions of a node in Drupal, you may want to query the database for the most recent version of each node and ignore all of the older versions. We can do this by grouping on the nid column and using the MAX operator to determine the maximum version:

```php
<?php
  $query = db_select('node', 'n');
  $nid_alias = $query->addField('n', 'nid');
  $query->groupBy($nid_alias);
  $ver_alias = $query->addExpression('MAX(vid)', 'max_vid');
  $result = $query->execute();
?>
```

You can also use expressions to perform mathematical expressions. For example, we can calculate how long it has been since a node was added to the system. We will extend this expression by adding a parameter that can be passed in to determine the starting time for the calculation:

```php
<?php
  $query = db_select('node', 'n');
  $nid_alias = $query->addField('n', 'nid');
  $query->groupBy($nid_alias);
  $elapsed_alias = $query->addExpression(
      ':start_date - created', 'elapsed_time',
      array(':start_date' => time()));
  $result = $query->execute();
?>
```

This query will return the number of seconds that have elapsed from the time the node was created until the time the query was run in the elapsed_time column. As discussed earlier, the parameters to the query are passed in as an associative array, which are used in the query when the query is executed.

Limiting the data returned

We saw in the previous section on static statements that you can limit the number of records that are returned by a query using the db_query_range method. With dynamic queries, you simply add a range statement to restrict which records are returned. The signature of the range method is as follows:

```
range($start = NULL, $length = NULL)
```

Let's extend our query for all nodes to return 20 records starting at record 40:

```php
<?php
  $query = db_select('node', 'n');
  $query->addField('n', array('nid', 'title'));
  $query->range(20, 60);
  $result = $query->execute();
?>
```

If you want to remove the range after you have added it, you can call the range method with no parameters.

 If you want automatic pagination of your queries, check out the `PagerDefault` query extender.

Dynamic query extensions

The DBTNG layer provides developers with the ability to extend the query functionality for Select statements. There are two query extensions that are shipped with core. These allow you to easily page records and enable users to easily sort data displayed in tables. We will look at each in detail next.

Paging records

In Drupal 6, paging was done using a `pager_query`. In Drupal 7, the easiest way to add pagination to your query is using the `PagerDefault` query extender. This takes care of automatically loading the current page from the page request to properly display the results for the current page. The extender can be added to the query by calling the `extend` method:

```php
<?php
  $query = db_select('node', 'n');
  $query->addField('n', array('nid', 'title'));
  $query = $query->extend('PagerDefault')->limit(20);
  $result = $query->execute();
?>
```

There are a couple of things to note in the previous code. After calling the `extend` method, you should make sure to reassign the query variable to the result of the `extend` statement. This is necessary because the extension wraps the original query object. The second thing to note is that the limit method is used to determine how many records should be displayed per page.

In order to avoid forgetting to reset the query variable, the Drupal best practice is to add the `PagerDefault` extension when the query is created. To use this best practice, we would rewrite the code above as:

```php
<?php
  $query = db_select('node', 'n')
          ->extend('PagerDefault')
          ->limit(20);
  $query->addField('n', array('nid', 'title'));
  $result = $query->execute();
?>
```

Using this method of adding the `PagerDefault` extension will guarantee that you will not forget to reassign the query.

Sorting data

Similar to the `PagerDefault` extension replacing the `pager_query` from Drupal 6, the new `TableSort` extension replaces the `tablesort_sql` method from Drupal 6. To use the `TableSort` extension, you simply add it as an extension. The extension will provide sorting capabilities for all fields that are defined for the query:

```php
<?php
  $query = db_select('node', 'n')->extend('TableSort');
   $query->addField('n', array('nid', 'title'));
  $result = $query->execute();
?>
```

Extensions can be stacked on top of each other so you can both sort and paginate a query. To use this functionality, simply call `extend` multiple times with the name of the extension to add.

Custom extensions

You can also create custom extensions if you find yourself needing to add advanced functionality to the queries. The complete instructions for building a custom extension is beyond the scope of this book. In essence, you will need to extend the `SelectQueryExtender` object, which is defined in the `select.inc` file that is located in the `/includes/database` folder. Additional information on building a custom extension can be found at: `http://drupal.org/node/508796`.

Adding conditions to a query

The last step in writing queries is to filter the data that is returned to present appropriate information to the user. Some common examples include showing a specific node, getting a list of nodes that a specific user created, getting a list of nodes that were created by a user after a specific date, and so on.

Conditions correlate to the WHERE clause of an SQL statement or a HAVING clause in a query with a GROUP BY clause. Conditions can be added to a query using either the condition method or the where method. The signatures of each method are as follows:

```
condition($field, $value = NULL, $operator = NULL)

where($snippet, $args = array())
```

The main difference between these two methods is that the condition method allows standard operations to be easily encoded. The where clause allows you to enter an arbitrary SQL snippet for the condition. The SQL snippet is not validated for consistency across databases so you should ensure that it is well supported if you want to publish your module to a wide audience. Let's look at each method in more detail.

Condition method

The condition method lets us specify the field, value, and operator to use in the condition. Most of the conditions you add should use this method. Let's look at a quick example where we filter our nodes to a specific user:

```php
<?php
  $query = db_select('node', 'n');
   $query->condition('uid', $uid);
  $result = $query->execute();
?>
```

If you do not provide an operator, Drupal will automatically interpret the condition as the = operator if a single value is provided. If an array of values is passed, Drupal will interpret the condition as an IN condition. So, the following code would return all nodes written by users, 5, 6, and 7:

```php
<?php
  $query = db_select('node', 'n');
   $query->condition('uid', array(5, 6, 7));
  $result = $query->execute();
?>
```

You can also specify a variety of other operators including: `'BETWEEN'`, `'IN'`, `'NOT IN'`, `'IS NULL'`, `'IS NOT NULL'`, `'LIKE'`, `'='`, `'<'`, `'>'`, `'>='`, `'<='`. These operators should be usable with all database drivers.

>
> Although you can use the `'IS NULL'` and `'IS NOT NULL'` operators in a `condition` statement, you can also use the `isNull` and `isNotNull` methods both of which accept one parameter, the name of the field to check.

You can also specify a second query as the value of a `condition` statement. This allows you to build a query with a subquery in it. This can be useful in certain complex queries.

Where method

If the available operators for the `condition` method do not satisfy your needs, you can use the `where` method, which allows you to include any valid SQL snippet as the condition. For example, if we want to run a comparison against the title field after converting it to lowercase, you can use the following snippet:

```php
<?php
  $query = db_select('node', 'n');
    $query->where('LOWER(title) = :title', 'test');
  $result = $query->execute();
?>
```

You can chain `where` clauses and `condition` clauses together so you can use them interchangeably depending on the complexity of your conditions.

Chaining conditions

Many times, you will need to add multiple conditions to a query to correctly filter your results. There are several methods of linking conditions together. You can link them with an AND, OR, or XOR.

When you apply multiple conditions to a query, they are automatically joined with an AND. Therefore, both conditions must evaluate to true for a record to be returned:

```php
<?php
  $query = db_select('node', 'n');
    $query->condition('uid', array(5, 6, 7));
  $query->condition('title', '%test%', 'LIKE');
  $result = $query->execute();
?>
```

The above query will return only records that were created by users 5, 6, and 7 and where title also contains the word test.

If you prefer to join the conditions with an OR or XOR, you will need to join them with a call to db_or or db_xor as shown in the following example:

```php
<?php
  $query = db_select('node', 'n');
  $query->condition(db_or()
    ->condition('uid', array(5, 6, 7));
    ->condition('title', '%test%', 'LIKE')
  );
  $result = $query->execute();
?>
```

This query will return all records that were created by users 5, 6, and 7 or that have a title that contains the word test.

Working with result sets

After you have run the query and received results, you can then retrieve the actual data from the result set. There are several different methods that can be used to retrieve data from the result set including fetch, fetchObject, fetchAssoc, fetchField, fetchAll, fetchAllAssoc, fetchAllKeyed, and fetchCol. These are all called as methods on the results object. For example, the following code will return all data from the query using the default fetch method defined in the options:

```php
<?php
  $result = db_query("SELECT nid, title FROM {node}");
  $all_data = $result->fetchAll();
?>
```

Let's look at each fetch method in detail now. While we review the functionality of the method, we will also match the function to the corresponding Drupal 6 functionality if applicable.

fetch and fetchAll

The fetch and fetchAll methods retrieve a single row or all rows in a result set respectively using the default fetch method defined in the query. In most cases, the default fetch method stores data into a standard object. The fetchAll method will store the records within an indexed array for retrieval.

The `fetch` method corresponds to the `db_fetch_object` method in most cases and the `fetchAll` method does not have a direct correlation in Drupal 6:

```php
<?php
  $query = db_select('node', 'n');
  $query->addField('n', array('nid', 'title'));
  $result = $query->execute();
  while ($node_data = $result->fetch()){
    //Do Something with the data
    //Data is accessed using
    //  $node_data->nid
    //  $node_data->title
  }
?>
```

These functions delegate their work to the `PDOStatement` methods of the same name.

fetchObject

The `fetchObject` method allows you to retrieve data into a custom class that you define. The class properties are filled out by PDO and then the constructor for the class is called. Additional information about this method can be found at: `http://drupal.org/node/315092`.

fetchAssoc

The `fetchAssoc` method loads a single record into an associated array so that it can be used as follows:

```php
<?php
  $query = db_select('node', 'n');
  $query->addField('n', array('nid', 'title'));
  $result = $query->execute();
  while ($node_data = $result->fetchAssoc()){
    //Do Something with the data
    //Data is accessed using
    //  $node_data['nid']
    //  $node_data['title']
  }
?>
```

fetchAllAssoc

The `fetchAllAssoc` method allows you to specify a field to use as the key for the resulting array. You can also specify the fetch method that should be used to retrieve each row. The method signature of the method is:

```
fetchAllAssoc($key, $fetch_style = PDO::FETCH_OBJ)
```

The `fetchAllAssoc` method can be an easy way to access the data from the result set if you know the IDs. The data can be used as follows:

```php
<?php
  $query = db_select('node', 'n');
  $query->addField('n', array('nid', 'title'));
  $result = $query->execute();
  $data = $result->fetchAllAssoc('nid',PDO::FETCH_OBJ);
  foreach ($result as $nid => $record){
    //Do Something with the data
    //Data is accessed using
    //   $record->nid
    //   $record->title
  }
?>
```

fetchField

The `fetchField` method is used to retrieve a single field from the result set. After the field is retrieved, the active row will be moved to the next row in the result. You can specify the column that should be received. The column should be specified by numeric index.

fetchAllKeyed

This method will return an associative array based on the passed-in key and value indexes. The method signature for this method is as follows:

```
fetchAllKeyed($key_index = 0, $value_index = 1)
```

The key and value indexes should be specified as numeric indexes within the fields. This method is really only useful if you have a query that returns data from only two columns. However, in that case, it can save programming time when creating lists of options and so on.

fetchCol

This method will return all values in a single column of a result set as an indexed array. You only need to specify the index of the column you wish to use in order to use this method. The signature is as follows:

```
fetchCol($index = 0)
```

Direct iteration

In addition to the methods described above, you can also directly iterate through the records in the results using a `foreach` loop as shown below:

```php
<?php
  $query = db_select('node', 'n');
  $query->addField('n', array('nid', 'title'));
  $result = $query->execute();
  foreach ($result as $record){
    //Do Something with the data
    //Data is accessed using
    //  $record->nid
    //  $record->title
  }
?>
```

In many cases, the direct iterator can be easier to read.

Tagging queries

DBTNG dynamic queries support the concept of tagging queries with additional information. This allows modules to determine which queries they want to work with and how they should be modified. You add a tag by simply calling the `addTag` method, which has the following signature:

```
addTag($tag)
```

The tag parameter is the name of the tag you want to add. You can check whether a particular tag has been added to the query using the `hasTag`, `hasAllTags`, or `hasAnyTag` methods.

There are several tags that are used in Drupal core, which may be useful to you in your modules. These include:

- `translatable` — indicates that the query contains translatable content.

- node_access — indicates that the query should be restricted based on permissions defined for the node. This restriction is done by Drupal automatically when it encounters the tag.
- pagerDefault — added by the PagerDefault query extender to indicate that the query is being paginated.
- tablesort — added by the TableSort query extender to indicate that the query is being sorted.

Adding these tags can make common tasks easier and make your queries more secure. If you would like to process a tag in your module, you can implement your changes in either hook_query_alter or hook_query_TAG_alter where the name of tag is inserted in the place of TAG. hook_query_TAG_alter allows you to restrict the invocation of your method to a specific tag, which can be more efficient if you only need to process a single tag.

insert statement syntax

Now that we have looked in depth at the various ways of selecting data using the Drupal 7 DBTNG layer, let's look into the insert queries. Insert queries are used to enter data into the database.

To create an insert statement, you start by calling the db_insert method. The signature of the db_insert method is:

```
db_insert($table, array $options = array())
```

The only required parameter is the name of the table you want to insert data into. For example, to create an insert statement for the node table, you would call:

```php
<?php
  $query = db_insert('node');
?>
```

Inserting single records

After the query has been created, you will need to specify which fields need to be inserted as well as the values for each field. This is done by calling the fields method of the insert query. You can call the fields method with an associative array that contains both the field names and the values for each field, as shown below:

```php
<?php
$query = db_insert('node')
```

```
    ->fields(array(
      'title' => 'Sample Node',
      'uid' => 1,
      'created' => REQUEST_TIME,
    ));
$nid = $query->execute();
?>
```

This will insert a node into the database that is created by user 1 at the current time and with a title of Sample Node. Note that, to actually insert the data into the table, you must call the execute method, which returns the ID of the last record that was inserted into the database if the record has an automatically incrementing field.

Inserting multiple records

If you need to insert more than one record at a time, you will need to specify the values independent of the fields by using the values method of the insert query object. The values method needs to be called once per record you want to insert. For example, we can create three nodes with names Sample 1 to Sample 3 using the following code:

```
<?php
$query = db_insert('node')->fields(array('title', 'uid', 'created'));
for ($i = 1; $i <= 3; $i++){
  $query->values(array("Sample $i", '1', REQUEST_TIME));
}
$query->execute();
?>
```

When you insert multiple records at one time, the return value of the execute method is not defined and should not be used.

Inserting records from another query

Sometimes, you will need to copy information from one table or query into another table. You can do this using an insert query by calling the from method of the insert query object. The from method takes a select query as an argument, which it executes and uses to fill the table you specified.

> When filling a table based on the results of another column, you should ensure that the order that data is received from the query matches the order of the fields for the table you are inserting data into.

Delayed inserts

The final capability of the insert query is the ability to delay an insert. This causes the database to execute the insert at some undetermined point in the future and return control to the calling program as quickly as possible. This can be useful when you are logging information or performing other operations where the data is not needed immediately. To mark the query as one that can be delayed, call the delay method on the query object. Remember that not all databases will support this method so you should not rely on it for optimizing performance in all cases.

update statement syntax

The update statement works similarly to the insert statement with some differences. You create an update statement by calling the db_update method. The db_update method has the following syntax:

```
db_update($table, array $options = array())
```

After you create the update statement, you will need to provide the fields that need to be updated as well as the new values for the fields. To specify the fields and values, you will call the fields method and pass an associative array to the method containing the field names and the new values for each field. You will also need to provide the conditions that records must match to be updated. To specify the conditions, you can use any of the functionality used in the select statements to build the conditions for the query.

Let's look at an example that updates the owner of all nodes to user 1 if the title of the node contains the word *admin* in it:

```php
<?php
$query = db_insert('node')
  ->fields(array(
    'uid' => 1
  ))
  ->condition('title', '%admin%', 'LIKE');
$num_updated = $query->execute();
?>
```

The result of the execute method for update statements is the number of rows that were updated as a result of the query.

merge statement syntax

A `merge` query attempts to automatically determine whether a record should
be inserted or updated depending on whether a record already exists in a
database matching a unique key for the table. Because many databases do not
implement merges in a standard method, the DBTNG layer delegates much of the
implementation to the database driver.

To create a `merge` statement, you begin by calling `db_merge`, which has the
following signature:

```
db_merge($table, array $options = array())
```

Just like the other methods we have looked at so far, you begin the query by passing
in the name of the table that you are working with. After you create the query, you
must tell Drupal how to determine whether a record already exists in the database or
not. This is done by calling the `key` method with an associative array with the name
of the field or fields that should be checked as well as the existing values that need
to be checked. Finally, you need to specify the values for each field that need to be
inserted or updated. This is done by calling the `fields` method with an associative
array much like we did in the `insert` and `update` methods.

The following example demonstrates either updating or adding a user depending
on whether or not the name field already exists in the database:

```php
<?php
$query = db_insert('user')
  ->key('name' => 'mnoble')
  ->fields(array(
    'name' => 'mnoble',
    'pass' => 'testPassword',
    'mail' => 'mnoble@drupalbyexample.com'
  ))
  $query->execute();
?>
```

If needed, you can also specify expressions to perform mathematical functions on
a field.

 A `merge` statement may or may not be atomic depending on the database
being used. Check your driver before relying on the statement being
executed in one step.

`merge` queries can be difficult to execute correctly. For additional information about `merge` queries, see the online documentation at `http://drupal.org/node/310085`.

delete statement syntax

If you need to delete a record from a table, you can use a `delete` query to remove the record. A `delete` statement is started by calling the `db_delete` method, which accepts the table to delete from much like the other queries we have looked at. The signature of the `db_delete` method is:

```
db_delete($table, array $options = array())
```

After creating the query, you need to specify the condition that should be used to determine which records should be deleted. You can use any of the condition functions we described earlier while talking about select statements.

Let's look at a simple example that deletes any node that has the word *delete* in the title.

```php
<?php
$query = db_insert('node')
  ->condition('title', '%delete%', 'LIKE');
$num_deleted = $query->execute();
?>
```

The `execute` method for a `delete` statement will return the number of records that were actually deleted by the query.

truncate statement syntax

The truncate statement will remove all records from a table. You can create a truncate query by calling `db_truncate` with the name of the table. For example, to remove all records from the node table, use the following code:

```php
<?php
$query = db_truncate('node');
$query->execute();
?>
```

Obviously, this method should be called sparingly and shouldn't be used unless you are truly sure you want to remove all records from a table.

Transaction support

The Drupal 7 DBTNG layer also supports transactions for database drivers that support transactions. If a driver does not support transactions, Drupal will automatically disable transaction functionality for you.

The key issue related to transactions in PHP is the potential for deadlocks due to multiple methods attempting to start transactions. If a transaction has been started in one method and a different method also attempts to start a transaction, the second transaction must wait until the first transaction completes until it can be started. Without proper protection, this can prevent the page load from completing. Thankfully, Drupal 7 protects against this behavior by providing the db_transaction method, which will allow the second function to acknowledge and utilize the transaction started in the first method.

To utilize this functionality, you should call db_transaction at the beginning of the method you want to have transaction support. As soon as the method exits, the transaction will be automatically closed. When the last method exits that was using transactions, all database operations enclosed in the transactions will be committed.

Master/slave replication

Drupal 7 now provides built-in support for setting up master/slave relationships for a database. This is done within the settings.php file. To specify a database connection that support master/slave relationships, you will need to define multiple targets for a single connection within your settings.php file.

Each database connection must have one default target that will be used in the event that none of the slave servers are available.

SQLite support

Also new in Drupal 7, is built-in support for SQLite. SQLite is a light-weight database where all of the data is stored in a single file on the server. The SQLite engine is also very compact.

Although, you wouldn't want to run a large high traffic site on a SQLite database, it can run smaller sites with lower traffic without any problems. You can also use SQLite to store data that you don't want in your main database. For more information on SQLite, you can see the official SQLite site at http://www.sqlite.org/.

Summary

In this chapter, we reviewed the changes to Drupal 7 related to interacting with the database. The new DBTNG layer introduced in Drupal 7 makes developing modules for Drupal much easier and makes the resulting code easier to read, understand, and debug.

If you need additional information about the new DBTNG layer, the online manual contains quite a lot of good information. The manual is available at: `http://drupal.org/node/310069`.

For more information on each function, you can also see the API reference information that is available in `http://api.drupal.org/api/group/database/7`.

In the next chapter, we will review the other changes to Drupal 7 for developers.

7
Drupal 7 for Developers

In the last chapter, we looked at the new DBTNG layer for Drupal 7, which controls how you interact with databases in Drupal. DBTNG is arguably the biggest and most important change for developers in Drupal 7. However, there are also numerous other changes that affect how module developers will interact with the system.

In this chapter, we will take a look at all of the key changes to the Drupal API. We will start by looking at the `.info` file changes that are required to make custom modules function properly as well as changes to the API related to getting information about modules. Next, we will look into changes related to the Drupal core system. After this, we will examine changes to the menu system before moving onto changes to the Form API and file uploads. Following the file handling APIs, we will consider the new Field API from a developer's perspective. We will wrap up by checking out changes to other areas including:

- Searching
- Tokens
- Triggers and Actions
- Image handling
- RDF
- Translation

We will conclude the chapter by talking about upgrading your Drupal 6 modules to work with Drupal 7.

.info file changes

A .info file is required by all modules in Drupal. The .info file gives Drupal information about your module. The .info file for modules is very similar to the .info files we looked at for installation profiles and themes. The big change to .info files is that you must now declare any associated PHP files that you plan on using from your module. Let's look at an example of a .info file for a fictional Drupal 7 Rocks module.

```
; $Id$
name = Drupal 7 Rocks
description = "Promotes the coolness of Drupal 7."
core = 7.x
package = Views
dependencies[] = Other
dependencies[] = panels
files[]  = drupal_7_rocks.module
files[]  = drupal_7_rocks.inc
files[]  = drupal_7_rocks.admin.inc
files[]  = includes/drupal_7_rocks.extra.inc
```

The structure of the file is the same as it was in Drupal 6; other than that the files array has been added and is now required. The files directive allows Drupal to dynamically load code from files more efficiently. It also allows you to place code that implements hooks outside of the main .module file.

When you convert your modules to Drupal 7, make sure to update your .info file to change the core version to 7.x and include all files that your module uses in the .info file.

Drupal hook changes

After you have updated your .info file, you can start to revise the code of your module. In this section, we will review some of the major changes to the general Drupal API before diving into specific key functional areas.

Hooks split by op code

In Drupal 7, several hooks from Drupal 6 have been split into multiple hooks based on the Drupal 6 op code. For example, the Drupal 6 hook_node_type: becomes hook_node_type_delete, hook_node_type_insert, and hook_node_type_update in Drupal 7. This makes the code implementing the hooks more efficient as well as making it easier for developers to easily find out which hooks can be implemented. The hooks that have been split in this manner include:

- hook_aggregator
- hook_block
- hook_comment
- hook_menu_link
- hook_node_type
- hook_search
- hook_user
- hook_nodeapi — this was split into hook_node_ hooks

More information about each of these hooks can be found at: http://api.drupal.org/api/7. To convert these hooks to Drupal 7, you will need to add hooks for any operation that you implemented in Drupal 6 and then move the implementation from the old hook to the new operation specific hook. After the move is done, you can remove the old Drupal 6 hook.

Other changed hooks

In addition to the methods that have been split based on operation code, there are several other core hooks, which have had their parameters changed. Let's look at each in detail.

hook_load

This hook is called when nodes are being loaded from the database. It is only called for the module that controls the nodes content type. In Drupal 7, the method signature changed from:

```
hook_load($node)
```

to:

```
hook_load($nodes)
```

The $nodes variable is now an array of nodes that can be acted upon so you no longer have to process each node one at a time, which can be much more efficient. For more information on this hook, see: http://api.drupal.org/api/function/hook_load/7.

hook_system_info_alter

This hook is called when the .info file for a module or file is being loaded into the system. A module or theme can implement this hook to override or define additional information about the module being loaded. In Drupal 7, the signature has changed from:

```
hook_system_info_alter(&$info, $file)
```

to:

```
hook_system_info_alter(&$info, $file, $type)
```

The new parameter $type indicates whether the .info file being loaded is for a module or a theme. You will receive a value of either 'module' or 'theme' when the hook is called.

hook_view

This hook is called during the display process for nodes. It can be used to add additional information to a node before it is rendered. In Drupal 7, the signature has been changed from:

```
hook_view($node, $teaser = FALSE, $page = FALSE)
```

to:

```
hook_view($node, $view_mode = 'full')
```

Rather than passing the teaser and page variables separately, which limited the number of page types that could be handled, Drupal 7 replaces it with a single variable called $view_mode. If your code was checking for teaser to be true in Drupal 6, you should now look for a view_mode of 'teaser'. The page view has been removed by default. However, you can use the 'full' view_mode to similar effect. Additional view modes are defined based on the entity type. To add additional view_modes programmatically, you can add them in the hook_entity_info method.

New hooks

Drupal 7 also introduces several new hooks that can be implemented by modules. Let's look at the signature of each new hook with a brief discussion of the use of that hook.

hook_admin_paths

```
hook_admin_paths
```

This hook defines which paths defined by a module should be considered as administrative paths. A theme may display administrative paths differently. For example, administrative paths can be displayed in the overlay or with a different theme. You should return an associative array with the path name as the key and the value TRUE for any path you want to be administrative. Paths can include wild cards.

hook_admin_paths_alter

```
hook_admin_paths_alter(&$paths)
```

This hook allows you to modify which paths are defined as administrative paths for paths that are defined by other modules. An associative array of all existing paths is passed to this method and you can alter it as needed.

hook_archiver_info

```
hook_archiver_info()
```

This hook allows you to define classes that can combine and extract multiple files into a single file that can optionally be compressed. For example, ZIP files and `tar.gz` files are both archive files that could be created with an archiver. To create an archiver class, you must implement the `ArchiverInterface`, which is defined in the `archiver.inc` file in the `includes` directory.

The return value for this hook is an associative array with the following keys:

- `class`: the class name of a class which implements the `ArchiverInterface`
- `extensions`: an array of file extensions that the class can handle
- `weight`: allows you to influence which archiver should be used if more than one archiver can handle a specific extension

hook_css_alter

```
hook_css_alter(&$css)
```

This hook allows you to modify which css files are rendered to the page. The `$css` variable is an array of all files and inline CSS which will be output keyed based on the filename of the file to be included. Inline CSS will not have a key in the array. You can either unset elements from the array or add new elements to the array as needed.

hook_dashboard_regions

```
hook_dashboard_regions()
```

This hook allows you to specify one or more regions that are eligible to be added to the dashboard. To add a region, you should return an array where the key is the ID of the region and the value is the description of the region. For example, the following code would return a new dashboard region called `drupal7rocks_ dashboard_region`. If your module name was drupal7rocks:

```
return array('drupal7rocks_dashboard_region'
        => "A sample region");
```

If you want to theme the region, you can add a method named theme_*region_name*() to handle the output.

hook_dashboard_regions_alter

```
hook_dashboard_regions_alter($regions)
```

This hook allows you to modify the regions created by other modules. The only real use for this is to remove regions that you do not want displayed to your site editors.

hook_date_formats

```
hook_date_formats()
```

As discussed earlier in the book, the date formats in Drupal have changed significantly. This hook allows you to define additional date formats that can be used within the system. Drupal expects you to return an array of formats. Each format consists of an array with three keys that are defined as follows:

*   type—the type of format to use. This is can be defined in either hook_date_format_types, created in the administrative interface, or reused from another module.

- `format` — the format which should be used when displaying the date. The format is defined according to the formatting options at: `http://php.net/manual/en/function.date.php`.

- `locales` — an array of languages that this format applies to. If your date format does not apply to a specific locale, you should leave this blank.

hook_date_formats_alter

```
hook_date_formats_alter(&$formats)
```

This hook allows you to override and change the date formats created by other modules. You can change the locales which apply, modify the date format, or completely remove the format.

hook_date_format_types

```
hook_date_format_types()
```

This hook allows you to define additional formats to the long, medium, and short date types that are defined within the core Drupal system programmatically. The return value for this hook should be an array of types where the key is the programmatic identifier and the value is a translatable label for the type. You should prefix any additional types you add using the name of your module to avoid conflicts. For example, the following code would add an `extra_long` format type to the system:

```php
<?php
function mymodule_date_format_types() {
  return array(
    'mymodule_extra_long' => t('Extra Long'),
  );
}
?>
```

hook_drupal_goto_alter

```
hook_drupal_goto_alter(&$path, &$options,
    &$http_response_code)
```

This hook allows you to influence a redirection that is performed by the `drupal_goto` function. You can modify any of the parameters passed to the hook to change the path, response code, or any of the options for the page that the user will be redirected to.

hook_library

```
hook_library()
```

This allows you to define reusable JavaScript or CSS libraries so they can be used throughout the system. For example, Drupal uses this mechanism to add jQuery and jQuery UI to the site as well as setting up JavaScript and CSS to handle vertical tabs on the site. After a library is defined, you can utilize it by calling `drupal_add_library`. Defining a library can be complex, so refer to: `http://api.drupal.org/api/function/hook_library/7` for more information.

hook_library_alter

```
hook_library_alter(&$libraries, $module)
```

Similar to other alter hooks, the `hook_library_alter` method allows you to change the libraries defined by other modules. This could be used to update a library to a newer version. However, care should be taken when doing this that backwards compatibility is maintained to avoid causing errors in modules that depend on a specific version of a library.

hook_modules_disabled

```
hook_modules_disabled($modules)
```

When you implement this module, you can react when other modules in the system are disabled. You can use this to perform additional logging or alter content that may have depended on the related modules.

 If you need to know when your own module is disabled, you should still implement `hook_disable`, which is only invoked on the module being disabled.

An array of modules being disabled is passed into the hook.

hook_modules_enabled

```
hook_modules_enabled($modules)
```

Similar to `hook_modules_disabled`, this hook allows you to take action when other modules are enabled. You can use this to enable enhanced functionality in your module if you don't want to force a dependency on another module. You can still implement `hook_enabled` to determine when your own module is enabled.

hook_modules_installed

```
hook_modules_installed($modules)
```

This hook allows you to take action when another module is installed in the system before it is enabled.

hook_modules_uninstalled

```
hook_modules_uninstalled($modules)
```

Like the previous three hooks, this hook allows you to detect when other modules change installation state. In this case, detecting when another module has been uninstalled.

hook_openid

```
hook_openid($op, $request)
```

This hook allows you to extend an OpenID request with additional information. The operation being performed is passed in as the $op variable. Currently, the only operation that is defined is 'request'. The request variable will contain an associative array with a list of parameters to be passed to the request. You may add, remove, or alter any of the parameters.

hook_openid_response

```
hook_openid_response($response, $account)
```

This hook is called after an OpenID request has been made and the response has been returned to your site. This allows you to process additional information returned from the OpenID server, possibly storing it locally in your database. This gives you the ability to retrieve information from the OpenID Attribute Exchange service.

For more information on OpenID, see the following resources:

* http://drupal.org/handbook/modules/openid
* http://openid.net

hook_path_delete

```
hook_path_delete($path)
```

This hook is called anytime a path within the system has been deleted. You can use this hook to update any content related to the path as needed.

hook_path_insert

```
hook_path_insert($path)
```

This hook is called whenever a path is inserted into the system. You can use this hook to update related content.

hook_path_update

```
hook_path_update($path)
```

This hook is called whenever a path is updated within the system. You can use this hook to update related content.

hook_registry_files_alter

```
hook_registry_files_alter(&$files, $modules)
```

Drupal 7 stores information about modules within a module registry in the database. Each file that is parsed by Drupal and included in the registry must be included in the $files array. A complete list of the modules that are being added to the registry is available in the modules array. In addition to the name of the module, all of the information from the .info module is included in the modules array. For more information about this hook, see: http://api.drupal.org/api/function/hook_registry_files_alter/7.

hook_overlay_child_initialize

```
hook_overlay_child_initialize()
```

This hook is called before a page is going to be displayed within the overlay window. This allows modules to alter their functionality as needed. For example, you may need to change the JavaScript or CSS files that are included or limit the data that is displayed.

hook_overlay_parent_initialize

```
hook_overlay_parent_initialize()
```

This hook is called when a page is displayed that might have an overlay displayed on top of it. This allows modules to alter their behavior to coexist with the overlay successfully. For example, you may need to add additional JavaScript or CSS to the page.

hook_shortcut_default_set

```
hook_shortcut_default_set($account)
```

This hook allows you to override the default shortcut set for a user account. This gives you the ability to define default shortcuts for users based on their role or other information in their profile.

 If the user has overridden their default shortcut set, the user's preferences will be respected and this method will not be called.

hook_system_info_alter

```
hook_system_info_alter(&$info, $file, $type)
```

You can use this information to change the information about a module that is normally stored within a module's `.info` file. The `$info` variable holds the contents of the `.info` file, which were read from the `.info` file. The `$file` variable includes the name and filename of the module or theme that is being read. The `$type` variable will be set to either 'module' or 'theme' depending upon the type of `.info` file being read.

hook_url_inbound_alter

```
hook_url_inbound_alter(&$path, $original_path,
    $path_language)
```

With this hook, you can perform aliasing of paths in the system. The `$path` variable should be set to the "real" path that Drupal recognizes. For example, `node/123` is a valid Drupal path. The `original_path` variable contains the path that was presented to the user. This path can be virtually anything depending on aliasing and processing by other modules. The `path_language` is set to the user's language so, you can have paths translated according to language.

System aliases are applied prior to calling this method, so you can also check the path for known aliases if you want.

hook_url_outbound_alter

```
hook_url_outbound_alter(&$path, &$options, $original_path)
```

This hook is similar to the previous hook. However, this method changes URLs before they are rendered to the user. The path variable contains the path to be rendered to the user. This can be altered as needed for your module. The options array contains additional fragments or query strings that are added to the URL at the end of processing. The original_path contains the internal system name of the path to be rendered.

hook_username_alter

```
hook_username_alter(&$name, $account)
```

This hook allows you to modify, typically obscuring, the username that is displayed to site visitors. You could also use this to alter names based on information in a third-party system. The $name variable is the name that will be displayed to site visitors. This can be altered as needed. The $account variable contains information about the account being displayed, which you can use as a source of information.

hook_xmlrpc_alter

```
hook_xmlrpc_alter(&$methods)
```

This hook is used in conjunction with the hook_xmlrpc method that has existed in Drupal since version 4.6. The new hook allows you to modify the methods defined by other modules. For more information about the structure of XML-RPC method definitions, see the hook_xmlrpc documentation at: http://api.drupal.org/api/function/hook_xmlrpc/7.

module_hook_info

```
module_hook_info()
```

This new method allows you to get a list of all hooks that have been defined within the system. You probably won't use this much in your custom modules, but it is essential for development-related modules. You may also want to use this if you need more information about a particular hook.

Removed methods

In addition to the methods that were added or modified, several methods and hooks have been removed in Drupal 7. Some of these have been replaced with other methods, and some are no longer necessary. Let's look at each quickly:

- `custom_url_rewrite_inbound` — this function has been replaced by `hook_url_inbound_alter`.

- `custom_url_rewrite_outbound` — this function has been replaced by `hook_url_outbound_alter`.

- `hook_footer` — this hook allowed you to add JavaScript and other information before the body was closed. You should now use `drupal_add_js` and `drupal_add_css` to achieve similar functionality.

- `hook_link`, `hook_link_alter` — these methods were removed as no longer being needed. If you were altering node links or comment links in the past, you should now utilize `hook_node_view_alter` and `hook_comment_view_alter`. You should generate any custom links you need using `hook_view`.

- `hook_ping` — this functionality has been removed from Drupal core. If you need this functionality, you will need to add a custom module to your site.

- `hook_profile_alter` — this method satisfies the same need that `hook_user_view` fulfills. If you were using `hook_profile_alter` in Drupal 6, you should use `hook_user_view` instead.

Menu system changes

Now that we have covered some of the general changes to the API in Drupal 7, we can begin looking at specific areas that have changed. Let's start by looking in more detail at how the menu system has changed in Drupal 7. The menu system is critical to making content appear on your site.

New hooks

Let's begin by looking at some of the new hooks, which relate to the menu system, that you may want to implement in your module:

hook_menu_active_handler_alter

```
hook_menu_active_handler_alter(&$router_item, $path = NULL)
```

This hook allows you to change how a menu is handled by the module system. You can set the following keys within the `router_item` array:

Property	Description
access	Set to false if the user should not be allowed to access the path or true if they are allowed to view the path.
file	The path to a file that can be included before the `path_callback` is executed.
page_callback	The callback to execute to generate the content of the path or perform needed functionality.
page_arguments	An array of arguments that should be passed to the `page_callback` when it is called.
delivery_callback	A function that should be called to render the content of the `page_callback` function.

hook_menu_contextual_links_alter

```
hook_menu_contextual_links_alter(&$links, $router_item,
    $root_path)
```

This hook can be used to add or change contextual links prior to rendering. Each link will contain a `title`, `href`, and `localized_options`. The `href` will be combined with the `localized_options` to build the actual links. The contextual links that are included in the links array are built by the `menu_contextual_links` method call.

hook_menu_delete

```
hook_menu_delete($menu)
```

This hook is called when a custom menu is deleted from the system. You can then take any needed actions within your module.

hook_menu_insert

```
hook_menu_insert($menu)
```

This hook is called when a new custom menu is added to the system. You can then take any needed actions.

hook_menu_local_tasks_alter

```
hook_menu_local_tasks_alter(&$data, $router_item, $root_path)
```

This hook is used to add additional tabs and/or actions to a page prior to rendering. For more information on creating tabs and actions correctly, see: http://api.drupal.org/api/function/hook_menu_local_tasks_alter/7

hook_menu_update

```
hook_menu_update($menu)
```

This hook is called every time a custom menu is updated. You can then alter any content as needed.

New methods

There are also a variety of methods that have been added to the Drupal core system, which you can utilize within your modules.

Method	Description
menu_contextual_links	Allows you to retrieve a list of contextual links for a specific module and path based on the local tasks that have been registered by the system.
menu_delete_links	Allows you to delete all of the links for a specific menu.
menu_get_active_menu_names	Returns the breadcrumbs for the current page from the site root to the current page.
menu_get_custom_theme	Allows you to retrieve the custom theme for a specific page.
menu_get_router	Returns the menu router that will be used to direct page requests to the proper module.
menu_links_clone	Duplicates a set of links so they can be used in another context.
menu_load_links	Returns an array of all links associated with a menu.

Method	Description
menu_local_actions	Returns a list of local actions that have been pre-rendered for display on the current page.
menu_main_menu	Returns an array of links to be rendered as the Main menu.
menu_reset_static_cache	Resets the Drupal menu cache so it will be rebuilt the next time the menu is accessed.
menu_secondary_menu	Returns an array of links to be rendered as the Secondary menu.
menu_set_active_menu_names	Sets or retrieves the active menu for the current page.
menu_set_custom_theme	Defines a custom theme to be used for the current page. This will allow the page to be rendered with a different appearance than the rest of the site.

Changed methods

Your module may also use some of the following methods that have been modified in Drupal 7.

menu_execute_active_handler

This method has been modified to accept a new optional parameter called $deliver with a default value of true. The $deliver variable determines whether the results of the menu handler should be rendered to the browser or returned to the calling function. Your existing modules should not need to change as a result of this change.

menu_get_names

This method will return a list of all menu names that have been defined within the system. It has been modified to remove the reset variable. If you were providing this variable, you should remove it.

menu_local_tasks

This method will return a list of tabs, actions, and the root path for the active page. This method has been modified to remove the $return_root variable, which was optional in Drupal 6. The root path will always be returned now. If you were passing the $return_root variable in your module, you should remove it in Drupal 7.

menu_router_build

This method builds the menu router so that it can be used later. The `$reset` method has been removed from the call. The menu router will now always be rebuilt when this method is called.

menu_tree_all_data

This method returns the raw data used to generate the menu tree. This method may contain data that is hidden so you should be careful where it is used. The method has been modified to rename the `$item` parameter to `$link` and adds a `$max_depth` parameter so you can control how much data is loaded.

menu_tree_data

This method returns the data used to render a menu. This method will not return menu items that are hidden. The `$result` parameter has been modified to become an array of links and has been renamed to `$links`.

menu_tree_page_data

This method returns menu information for a specific page. The method has been modified to add a `$max_depth` parameter that controls how much data should be returned.

Removed methods

The following methods have been removed from the Menu API. If your code uses them, you will need to replace them with the equivalent function.

- `menu_get_active_menu_name` — this method has been removed. You can use `menu_get_active_menu_names` for similar functionality.

- `menu_path_is_external` — this method has been renamed to the `url_is_external` method.

- `menu_primary_links` — this method has been replaced by the `menu_main_menu` method.

- `menu_secondary_links` — this method has been replaced by the `menu_secondary_menu` method.

- `menu_set_active_menu_name` — this method has been removed. You can use `menu_set_active_menu_names` for similar functionality.
- `menu_valid_path` — this method has been renamed to `drupal_valid_path`. The `$form_item` parameter has also been renamed to `$path` and the `$dynamic_allowed` parameter was added. The `$dynamic_allowed` parameter is used to restrict whether or not paths with wildcards should be treated as valid.

Form API changes

Now that we have reviewed the changes to the menu system, let's look at changes to the Form API. There are several new methods in Drupal 7 that make it easier to work with Drupal forms as well as making forms more powerful.

New Form API hooks

The Form API has several new hooks that allow you to influence the building and display of forms.

hook_element_info

```
hook_element_info()
```

This hook allows you to define additional element types that should become available for use within the Form API. The return value of this API is an associative array containing information about the element to be defined. For a complete list of keys that should be provided, see the online documentation at: http://api.drupal.org/api/function/hook_element_info/7.

This hook is derived from the Drupal 6 `hook_elements` method. If you used `hook_elements` in your Drupal 6 modules, you can convert the module to use `hook_element_info` in Drupal 7.

hook_element_info_alter

```
hook_element_info_alter(&$type)
```

This hook is used to alter the information returned by other modules in the previous hook. This allows you to change the custom elements defined by other modules.

hook_form_system_theme_settings_alter

```
hook_form_system_theme_settings_alter(&$form, &$form_state)
```

This hook is related both to the Form API as well as theming. This method allows you to alter the configuration form for a custom theme to add additional options to the theme.

hook_node_prepare

```
hook_node_prepare($node)
```

This hook is called on nodes before they are shown in an add or edit form. This allows you to set default values for a node or alter information about a node before a user changes it.

Changed methods

Let's look at the methods whose method signatures have changed in Drupal 7.

form_type parameter renamed

There are several methods in the Form API that begin with `form_type`, for example, `form_type_checkbox_value`. The parameters for these methods have all been changed. Instead of passing `$form` and `$edit` parameters, Drupal will now pass `$element` and `$input` parameters. However, the meaning of these parameters is unchanged from Drupal 6, so all you will need to do is rename the parameters in your code.

drupal_rebuild_form

This function retrieves a form, adds it to the cache, and then processes it. The functions have been changed by removing the `$args` argument. This was not really used in Drupal 6 so it has been removed.

drupal_redirect_form

This function will redirect the user to a specific URL after the form is processed. In Drupal 7, the parameters for the method have been combined into a single parameter called `$form_state`. The new `$form_state` parameter has several keys in the array that determine how the function behaves including:

- `redirect` — the destination to redirect to or FALSE to prevent redirection
- `no_redirect` — if true, the function that originally defined the form disallows redirection. This value should never be modified
- `programmed` — if this is set to true, the form submission was invoked programmatically so a redirect should not be done to avoid breaking the calling script
- `rebuild` — if true, the form should be rebuilt without redirection

form_builder

This function will build a form by adding the required properties to elements and setting input data appropriately. It will also execute process handlers that have been defined for elements. In Drupal 7, the `$form` parameter has been renamed `$element` to be more descriptive, but the base functionality remains the same.

form_set_error

This method adds errors to form elements. The method signature has been changed to:

```
form_set_error($name = NULL, $message = '',
    $limit_validation_errors = NULL)
```

The `$reset` parameter from Drupal 6 has been dropped and the `$limit_validation_errors` parameter has been added. This can be used to limit which elements should be validated. For more information on properly handling these values, see the documentation at:

http://api.drupal.org/api/function/form_set_error/7.

form_type_image_button_value

This method is used to determine the value of an image button. In Drupal 7, the `$edit` parameter has been changed to `$input` similar to other `form_type` methods. The `$form_state` has also been added to handle browser-specific quirks.

New methods

In addition to the methods that changed for form generation, Drupal 7 also adds several new methods to the Form API.

- `drupal_build_form` — this method builds a form or retrieves it from the cache if possible. The form is then processed, validated, and submitted if proper input has been provided. The signature of the method is:

  `drupal_build_form($form_id, &$form_state)`

  Input should be input key of the `$form_state` parameter.

- `drupal_form_submit` — similar to the previous method, this method builds a form or returns it from the cache, processes it, and validates it. However, it is not actually submitted. Instead, any errors that occur are returned to the user.

- `form_clear_error` — as the name implies, this method clears all errors on all form elements.

- `form_pre_render_conditional_form_element` — this method is used to perform basic theming for checkboxes and radio buttons that are displayed within a form.

- `form_pre_render_fieldset` — this method will create elements for child elements within a fieldset so that the children can be properly rendered in the display.

- `form_process_container, form_process_date, form_process_fieldset, form_process_password_confirm, form_process_radios, form_process_tableselect, form_process_text_format, form_process_vertical_tabs, form_process_weight` — these methods all generate elements for display within a form. Generally, you will not need to call these methods directly. Instead, you will call `drupal_get_form` or related methods to build a form.

- `form_state_defaults` — this method builds default values for the `form_state` variable, which is passed throughout several form generation methods.

- `form_state_values_clean` — this method removes elements that the Drupal Form API adds to forms prior to processing by modules.

Removed methods

Lastly, let's look at the Form API methods that have been removed.

- `drupal_execute` — this method was replaced by `drupal_form_submit`. You can replace any custom code you had, which called `drupal_execute` with `drupal_form_submit` directly.

- `drupal_render_form` — this method has been removed from Drupal 7. You can replace this functionality with the similar `theme_form` method.

- `expand_date` — this method was used to display a set of selection boxes that allowed the user to set the month, day, and year of a date. It has now been replaced with `form_process_date`.

- `expand_password_confirm` — this method was used to display a password field as well as a confirmation box to ensure that the password was entered properly. This method has now been replaced by `form_process_password`.

- `expand_radios` — this method was used in Drupal 6 to display a set of radio buttons in a form. This method has been replaced in Drupal 7 with `form_process_radios`.

- `form_clean_id` — this method was used in Drupal 6 to process CSS IDs. Since the method was misnamed in Drupal 6, it has been renamed to `drupal_css_id` in Drupal 7.

- `form_expand_ahah` — this method has been renamed in Drupal 7 to `form_process_aha`.

- `hook_elements` — this hook was renamed to `hook_element_info` in Drupal 7.

- `process_weight` — this hook was renamed to `form_process_weight` in Drupal 7.

File handling system

Let's move on now to the file handling system. As we have seen in previous chapters, the user interface for the file handling system was changed significantly. For example, a Drupal 7 site can now use both private and public files within the same site. We can also now add files to our site using file fields in addition to the file uploads that were provided in previous versions of Drupal. To enable these changes, the APIs related to file handling were significantly revised.

New file hooks

Let's start by looking at the new hooks that your modules may want to implement in Drupal 7.

hook_file_copy

```
hook_file_copy($file, $source)
```

This hook is called after a file has been copied in the system. You can use this hook to update related information or add new information to the database.

hook_file_delete

```
hook_file_delete($file)
```

This hook is called when a file has been deleted. You can use this to clean up associated information in the database.

hook_file_insert

```
hook_file_insert(&$file)
```

This hook allows you to respond when a new file is created in the system. You can use this information to import content, add associations, and so on.

 This hook is called both when files are created when they are copied as well as when they are uploaded, so make sure your code is appropriate for both situations.

hook_file_load

```
hook_file_load($files)
```

This hook allows you to add additional information about files that have been loaded by Drupal into the files array. To do this, you can add additional properties to each entry within the files array. You can utilize this information later during the rendering process or in other functions within your module.

hook_file_mimetype_mapping_alter

```
hook_file_mimetype_mapping_alter(&$mapping)
```

This hook allows you to change the mimetypes that are used by the file system. Changing the mimetype changes how a file is handled by the browser. For example, you can tell a browser to handle a .csv file as plain text by assigning a mimetype of text/plain or you can have it treated as an Excel file by assigning a mimetype of application/Excel. To make changes to the mappings, you should alter the mapping parameter directly. The mapping array contains two nested arrays within it, a mimetypes array that contains a list of all available mimetypes, and an extensions array that maps each extension to the name of the mimetype which should be used. For more information see:

http://api.drupal.org/api/function/hook_file_mimetype_mapping_alter/7 and http://api.drupal.org/api/function/file_default_mimetype_mapping/7.

hook_file_move

```
hook_file_move($file, $source)
```

This hook is called after a file is moved within the system. You can use this method to update your content based on the new location if needed, but you cannot prevent the move from occurring.

hook_file_references

```
hook_file_references($file)
```

This hook is used to determine which modules are using a particular file. This information is then used by Drupal to determine whether or not a file is in use and whether or not it can be deleted. If you are using the file, you should return an array with your module name as a key with a value of the number of times the file is used.

hook_file_update

```
hook_file_update(&$file)
```

This hook is called when an existing file is changed in the system by calling file_save. You can use this hook to update related content. For example, you may need to re-import the contents of the file, modify titles, and so on.

hook_file_url_alter

```
hook_file_url_alter(&$uri)
```

This hook is called anytime the `file_create_url` method is called, and it gives you the ability to rewrite the output URL. You should ensure that the implementation of this hook executes very quickly because the hook can be called very frequently due to the `file_create_url` method being executed for each JavaScript and CSS file that is added to the page.

hook_file_validate

```
hook_file_validate(&$file)
```

This hook is used to validate the file. You can perform validation based on any of the properties of the file object that is passed in including the filename of the file. You should return an array of errors that you encounter. Each error should be a translated string that can be presented to the user. If you don't detect any problems, you should return an empty array.

Changed hooks

In addition to the new hooks that you can implement, the `hook_file_download` hook was also modified to accept a URI parameter rather than a file path. This allows you to enforce additional permissions on file downloads and specify additional http headers to be used when downloading a file.

New and changed methods

To support the new file capabilities, a variety of new methods have been added to the backend File API and several methods have been revised for improved functionality and usability. You can utilize these methods from your modules.

PHP method wrappers

A variety of methods that are built into PHP have been extended in Drupal to handle stream wrappers. These functions add support for stream wrappers, but do not change the core behavior of the functions. A complete list of these functions follows:

- `drupal_chmod`—allows you to change the permissions of a file or directory. The default permissions are loaded based on system variables that give read access to everyone and write permissions to the web server group. You can also specify specific permissions to set.

- `drupal_dirname` — returns the directory name that contains the given path.

- `drupal_mkdir` — creates a directory on the server. Extended to use default permissions set within Drupal and to allow stream wrappers to be used.

- `drupal_realpath` — returns the absolute path of a file or directory. This method is compatible with stream wrappers.

- `drupal_tempnam` — creates a temporary file with a unique name and then returns a URI for use.

File IO

Obviously, a key need in the File API is the ability to read and write information to and from files. In Drupal 7, the API changed to handle both managed files and unmanaged files. Managed files are controlled by Drupal and have information stored in the database about them. In Drupal 6 and before, all files were treated as unmanaged. Therefore, you will find that many of the Drupal 6 functions have been renamed by adding _unmanaged to the filename and a new method has been added that will handle managed files. As we go through the functions, we will point out cases where this change has been made.

- `file_copy` and `file_unmanaged_copy` — as the name implies, this function handles copying files on the server. After a file is copied, `hook_file_copy` will be called on all modules.

- `file_delete`, `file_unmanaged_delete`, and `file_unmanaged_delete_recursive` — these functions will delete a file from the server and delete the related database record. Before deleting the file, Drupal will call `hook_file_references` unless the new force parameter has been set to true. After the deletion completes, `hook_file_delete` will be called.

- `file_move` and `file_unmanaged_move` — these methods move a file within the file system and update the database record accordingly. `hook_file_move` will be called after the move has been completed.

- `file_load` — this method is used to load a file object from the database so that it can be passed to other functions for usage. The file is loaded based on its file ID.

- `file_load_multiple` — similar to the `file_load` method, this method will load a list of files from the database based on a set of conditions.

- `file_save` — this method will either save a new file to the database, or update an existing database record if the file already exists within the database.

- `file_save_data` and `file_unmanaged_save_data` — these methods will write data to a file within the file system. If a database entry does not already exist for the file, a new file entry will be created.

File information

The File API also provides several new and changed methods that provide information about the file system.

- `file_prepare_directory` — this method will ensure that a directory exists and that it can be written. If the directory does not exist, Drupal will attempt to create it.

- `file_scan_directory` — this method lists all of the files that are located in a specific directory. The method signature has been revised to combine the nomask, callback, recurse, and key parameters into a new options parameter, which is an array of options that tell the method how to behave. A new `min_depth` option has also been added.

- `file_space_used` — this method allows you to determine how much disk space is being used by either a specific user or in the entire file system. Drupal 7 adds a new status flag so you can determine which types of files are included in the check.

- `file_validate` — this method checks to ensure that a file matches a set of criteria defined by one or more validators that are passed to the file.

Stream wrapper implementations

Drupal 7 has also added the concept of stream wrappers that allow the system to handle local and remote files and resources in a consistent manner. This extends the stream wrapper functionality provided by PHP.

Streams are referred to using the format scheme://target, similar to the mechanism used for URLs.

- `file_directory_path` — this method allows you to retrieve the path to the files directory. Since Drupal 7 can now handle multiple file directories each with a different scheme, you now need to pass the scheme name to the method. This allows you to get the path for public, private, temporary, or any other schemas within the system that are returned by `file_get_stream_wrappers`.

- `file_get_stream_wrappers` — this method returns a list of all stream wrappers that have been defined within Drupal.

- `file_stream_wrapper_get_class` — with this method, you can get the class name that handles a specific stream wrapper class so that the implementation class can be instantiated.

- `file_stream_wrapper_get_instance_by_scheme` — similar to the previous method, this method will return an instance of the class that should be used to work with a given stream wrapper schema. When using this method, the class will be instantiated for you.

- `file_stream_wrapper_get_instance_by_uri` — this method can be used when you have a URI to a file rather than just the schema. The class implementing the stream wrapper schema will be returned for you.

- `file_stream_wrapper_uri_normalize` — this method prepares a URI for usage by removing:

    ◦ The wrapper's directory path
    ◦ Trailing slashes from the target
    ◦ Extra leading slashes from the target

  You should use this method when manually creating URIs to streams.

- `file_stream_wrapper_valid_scheme` — this method performs a check to ensure that a scheme has been registered within Drupal and that a handler exists that can work with the scheme.

URI and URL handling

To allow site visitors to access the files stored on the site, Drupal includes the ability to generate URLs and URIs that can be presented to site visitors so that they can download information. Many of the functions in Drupal 6 related to creating URLs have been modified to take a URI rather than a path to be compatible with stream wrappers. Other changes and new methods include:

- `file_build_uri` — creates a URI to the default public files location. This can be used when working with unmanaged files or giving the user access to public files.

- `file_uri_scheme` — this new function parses a URI and returns just the schema for use in other functions.

- `file_uri_target` — this new function parses a URI and returns just the target for use in other functions.

.htaccess file protection

A common way of protecting files on a web server is with the use of `.htaccess` files, which in addition to other options, control how Apache web servers serve files to site visitors. Starting with Drupal 7, Drupal has added several methods to work with `.htaccess` files.

- `file_create_htaccess` — this method will create a `.htaccess` file in the specified directory. The directory will be made either private or public depending on the state of the private parameter that is passed to the method. The directory to be protected can be specified either with the scheme name or with the full path to the directory.

- `file_ensure_htaccess` — this method makes sure that public, private, and temporary directories all have properly setup `.htaccess` files within them.

Removed methods

Given the number of methods that have been added to the File API in Drupal 7, it should be unsurprising that some methods from the Drupal 6 API are no longer needed and have been removed. These include:

- `file_check_directory` — this method has been removed and replaced with `file_prepare_directory`.

- `file_check_location` — this functionality had limited usage and has been removed. Similar functionality can be accomplished using stream wrappers.

- `file_check_path` — this functionality checked to see if a file was a directory or path. This functionality can now be handled with stream wrapper functionality.

- `file_create_path` — this can now be accomplished using `file_prepare_directory` or `file_directory_path`.

- `file_directory_temp` — this functionality is no longer needed. Instead, you can call `file_directory_path` and specify the temporary schema.

- `file_set_status` — this functionality was used in Drupal 6 to convert temporary files to permanent files. You can now simply change the status and call `file_save`.

Field API

The new field functionality is an extremely important change in Drupal 7 and the API was heavily modified to support this new functionality. Unfortunately, there is no space in this book to look at each new method in detail due to the sheer number of new hooks and methods within the Field API. Instead, let's look at the major concepts and subsections within the Field API. For a complete reference on the methods defined within the Field API, see: `http://api.drupal.org/api/group/field/7`.

Entities

Entities represent objects within Drupal that fields can be attached to. Entities must have a controller for them that is a class implementing the `DrupalEntityController` interface. The controller is responsible for loading entities and handling operations for the entity. Common built-in entities include nodes and users. Additional information about an entity can be defined using `hook_entity_info` and `hook_entity_info_alter`. You can react to entities being loaded using `hook_entity_load`.

Field types

Field types are used to define types of information that can be used as a field. Drupal defines field types including Boolean, Decimal, Integer, Text, File, Image, Term reference, and so on. In addition to these built-in types, you can define your own types using the Field API. To define a type within a module, you will implement `hook_field_info`, which defines the bulk of the information about a field type including:

- A label and description for the field type
- Settings for the field type that apply to all instances of a field regardless of the entity they are attached to
- Instance settings for the field type that can vary based on the entity that they are attached to
- The default widget that should be used when the field is displayed in a form for editing purposes
- The default formatter that should be used when displaying the value of the field within the pages of the site

We will discuss widgets and formatters in more detail shortly. If you would like to alter the definition of a field type created by another module, you can do so using `hook_field_alter`.

Field instances

To use a field, an instance of the field must be created and it must be attached to a valid entity. The behavior of an instance can be customized using the instance-specific settings. Although you can create fields without attaching them to bundles, it is typically more useful to attach them to a bundle right away. You can programmatically add and remove fields using the following methods: `field_create_field`, `field_create_instance`, `hook_field_create_field`, `hook_field_create_instance`, `field_delete_field`, `field_delete_instance`, `hook_field_delete_field`, and `hook_field_delete_instance`. The instance methods will attach or detach the field from a bundle in addition to creating or removing the field. The hook methods allow you to respond to fields being added or deleted by other modules or by site administrators.

Field bundles

Field bundles are used to group fields when they are attached to entities. In the Drupal user interface, bundles translate to content types. A bundle is defined by the base entity type and the name of the field bundle. Bundles can be controlled programmatically using the following methods within the Field API: `field_attach_create_bundle`, `hook_field_attach_create_bundle`, `field_attach_delete_bundle`, `hook_field_attach_delete_bundle`, `field_attach_rename_bundle`, and `hook_field_attach_rename_bundle`.

Displaying fields in forms with field widgets

Widgets are used to display fields within a form. A widget can range from a simple text field that the user can type information into, to complex fields that display calendar controls to site users with complex JavaScript. Really, a widget can be nearly anything you can imagine. A field can either use a custom widget or one of the built-in widgets defined by Drupal. You can create new widgets using `hook_field_widget_info` and you can modify the widgets defined by other modules using `hook_field_widget_info_alter`. These methods are used to define what field types the widget supports, additional settings that can be used for the widget, and the behaviors that should be used for the widget.

The widgets for an entity are added to a form during a call to `field_attach_form`. You can alter this process using `hook_field_attach_form`.

Displaying field data

Field information is displayed within your site using formatters. A formatter takes the raw data from the field and converts it into a structure suitable for theming. For example, the core file field offers the following formatters:

- Generic file
- Table of files
- URL to file

Formatters are defined within `hook_field_formatter_info`, and the formatters defined by other modules can be modified using `hook_field_formatter_info_alter`.

Before the field data is sent to the field formatter, it is first prepared by calling `hook_field_prepare_translation` and `hook_field_prepare_view`. These methods give you an opportunity to modify the raw data before it is sent to the formatter. The actual formatting of the object takes place in two stages. First, `hook_field_formatter_prepare_view` is called and then `hook_field_formatter_view`. The `hook_field_formatter_prepare_view` call can be used to load additional information needed during the actual formatting stage.

Saving, retrieving, and deleting field data

Field data is stored in the database using the Field Storage API. The Field Storage API is also used to store information about fields and field instances. The default Field Storage mechanism uses SQL to store information into the Drupal database, however, the Storage API is designed in such a way that you can replace the backend storage system to store data in any other type of repository including files, cloud-based databases, or remote systems accessed by API. You can define new storage engines using `hook_field_storage_info` or modify existing storage engines using `hook_field_storage_info_alter`. For more information on creating custom storage engines, see: `http://api.drupal.org/api/group/field_storage/7`.

Individual field information for a specific entity instance can be read from the database using `field_attach_load`. If your entity is using revisions, you can load information for a specific revision using `field_attach_load_revision`. You can react to data being loaded using `hook_field_attach_load`. Field data is stored in the database using `field_attach_insert` and `field_attach_update`. These also have associated hooks that are called when they are occur. Finally, data can be removed using `field_attach_delete` and `field_attach_delete_revision`. Again, the associated `hook_field_attach_delete` hook can be used to detect and react when field information is removed from the database.

Getting information about fields

Drupal also provides methods to load additional information about fields, field bundles, field formatters, and field widgets from your modules. These include:

- `field_info_bundles`
- `field_info_field`, `field_info_fields`, `field_info_by_id`
- `field_info_field_settings`, `field_info_field_types`
- `field_info_formatter_settings`, `field_info_formatter_types`
- `field_info_instance`, `field_info_instances`, `field_info_instance_ settings`
- `field_info_storage_settings`, `field_info_storage_types`
- `field_info_widget_settings`, `field_info_widget_types`

The information about fields is cached in the database to improve performance. You can clear the cache programmatically by calling `field_info_cache_clear`, which will cause the cache to be automatically rebuilt. No actual data is removed when calling this method.

Node access and permission changes

Several changes were made to the node access system and permission system to make it easier to make Drupal more secure. Let's look at the new features that have been added first.

Added methods

The Node API has been extended to include several new methods to give you more information and better control over the permission system.

hook_node_access

This hook allows you to influence whether or not a particular operation can be performed by a user on a given node. You are passed the node being accessed as well as the account performing the action. You are also given one of four possible operations: create, delete, update, or view. You should return one of the following constants:

- `NODE_ACCESS_ALLOW` if the operation is allowed
- `NODE_ACCESS_DENY` if the operation should be prevented
- `NODE_ACCESS_IGNORE` if your module does not care one way or the other

This hook takes the place of the old `hook_access` module from Drupal 6.

hook_node_access_records_alter

Similar to `hook_node_access`, this hook allows you to change the permissions for a node before they are written to the database. This hook is called after `hook_node_access_records`, which remains unchanged from Drupal 6, and allows you to modify the allowable records for a node before they are written to the database.

hook_node_grants_alter

This hook allows you to add or remove grants for a user that have been set in `hook_node_grants` or by other modules in `hook_node_grants_alter`. This allows you to apply advanced business logic to your permission system.

hook_user_cancel

This hook is called when a user cancels his/her own account. The cancellation method is passed to the hook with information about the account being canceled and the information entered by the user when they canceled the account.

hook_user_cancel_methods_alter

Using this hook, you can add, change, or remove the cancellation methods that are available to the administrators and optionally to users. This supports the new functionality for allowing users to delete their own accounts in Drupal 7.

hook_user_role_delete, hook_user_role_insert, and hook_user_role_update

This set of hooks allows you to react when a role has been added, removed, or changed within Drupal. This is especially important if your module adds supplemental data to the roles. In all cases, the role being affected is passed to the hook.

node_list_permissions

This helper method will return a list of all permissions that apply to a given type of node.

node_permissions_get_configured_types

This method will return a list of all node types that use the permission system. Unless a module has specifically overridden this behavior, all node types will use the permission system. For more information on overriding this behavior, see: `http://api.drupal.org/api/function/node_permissions_get_configured_types/7`.

user_role_permissions

This method will return an array of permissions that are active for the role or roles that have been passed in.

user_role_grant_permissions, user_role_change_permissions, and user_role_revoke_permissions

These methods allow you to add, modify, or remove permissions from a user role respectively. You can use these methods to programmatically set permissions for roles within your modules.

Changed methods

The only key change to the methods within the permission system is that `hook_perm` has been renamed `hook_permission`. However, the actual functionality has remained unchanged.

Text filter changes

To support the changes to text formats in Drupal 7, the Drupal API has been extended to allow modules to have additional interaction with the filter system. Modules can now define filters, alter existing filters, and handle filters being added, deleted, or changed. Let's look at each of the new hooks in more detail now.

hook_filter_format_delete

```
hook_filter_format_delete($format, $fallback)
```

This hook allows you to react when a filter has been deleted from the system. If any content that you are maintaining with your modules uses the format which is being deleted, you should update the content to use a new format. The fallback format is guaranteed to be valid.

hook_filter_format_insert

```
hook_filter_format_insert($format)
```

This hook allows your module to react when a new filter format has been created. You can use this opportunity to update any content you manage for the new format or any other options you deem necessary.

hook_filter_format_update

```
hook_filter_format_update($format)
```

This hook is called any time a filter format is updated within Drupal. If you have cached any processing of your content, you can use this opportunity to update your cache or do any additional actions that may be needed.

hook_filter_info

```
hook_filter_info()
```

With this hook, you can define additional filters that can be used to modify the site content that has been entered by users before it is redisplayed to site visitors.

hook_filter_info_alter

```
hook_filter_info_alter(&$info)
```

With this hook, you can modify filter definitions created by other modules. For example, you can change settings or even alter the function that processes the filter.

Removed methods

`hook_filter`, `hook_filter_tips`—these functions have been replaced by the new filter functionality described above.

Taxonomy changes

The taxonomy system has also been revised to work with the Field API and to give developers more hooks to interact with.

hook_taxonomy_term_delete

```
taxonomy_term_delete($term)
```

This hook is invoked when a taxonomy term is removed from the database. You can use this hook to update any content related to the term.

hook_taxonomy_term_insert

```
hook_taxonomy_term_insert($term)
```

This hook is invoked when a taxonomy term is added to the database. You can use this hook to update any content related to the term.

hook_taxonomy_term_load

```
hook_taxonomy_term_load($terms)
```

This hook is called when one or more terms are loaded from the database. You can alter or add information to the terms within this hook. You should ensure that functionality executed within this hook executes quickly and that it does not interfere with the Drupal taxonomy cache. For more information, see: `http://api.drupal.org/api/function/hook_taxonomy_term_load/7`.

hook_taxonomy_term_update

```
hook_taxonomy_term_update($term)
```

This hook is invoked when a taxonomy term is modified within the system. You can use this hook to update any content related to the term.

hook_taxonomy_vocabulary_delete

```
hook_taxonomy_vocabulary_delete($vocabulary)
```

You can use this hook to detect when an entire vocabulary has been deleted from the system, so you can update your content as needed.

hook_taxonomy_vocabulary_insert

    hook_taxonomy_vocabulary_insert($vocabulary)

When this hook is called, you know that a new vocabulary has been inserted in the system and you can adjust your content as needed.

hook_taxonomy_vocabulary_load

    hook_taxonomy_vocabulary_load($vocabularies)

A module can implement this hook to add information to the list of vocabularies that have been loaded by Drupal. You can add additional information to a vocabulary or alter existing information as needed.

hook_taxonomy_vocabulary_update

    hook_taxonomy_vocabulary_update($vocabulary)

This hook is called when a vocabulary is updated within the system and saved to the database. You can then update your content as needed based on the information in the vocabulary.

Removed methods

hook_term_path — this method has now been removed. To achieve the same functionality, you can use the new hook_url_alter method to change the path of taxonomy content.

Searching changes

Similar to other Drupal APIs, the Search API has been modified in Drupal 7 to make it easier for developers to use and interact with. Several methods have also been modified for consistency with other Drupal APIs.

Added methods

Several new hooks have been added to the API to allow your modules to provide additional information to the search system, allow you to modify the search process, and allow you to modify how the results are returned to the user.

hook_search_access

```
hook_search_access()
```

This hook allows you to define which permissions are necessary to access your custom search defined within hook_search_info. Then you can define which roles have access to the permission.

hook_search_admin

```
hook_search_admin()
```

With this hook, you can add additional elements to the administration form for the Search settings. You can then use these new properties during custom searches. The return value of this hook is an array of form elements. For more information, see: http://api.drupal.org/api/function/hook_search_admin/7.

hook_search_execute

```
hook_search_execute($keys = NULL)
```

This hook performs a search that has been defined in hook_search_info. This is a powerful method of getting a search to behave exactly the way you want and take advantage of improved search functionality. For more information, see: http://api.drupal.org/api/function/hook_search_execute/7.

hook_search_info

```
hook_search_info()
```

This hook allows you to create a custom search tab for your module on the search page. The search will then be executed by hook_search_execute. For more information on building a complete search system, see: http://api.drupal.org/api/group/search/7.

hook_search_reset

```
hook_search_reset()
```

This hook is called at the beginning of the search indexing process if the entire index is going to be rebuilt. If you use hook_update_index, you should reset your index at this time.

hook_search_status

```
hook_search_status()
```

This hook is used to inform the Search API of how many nodes are left to be indexed. You should return an associative array with two keys—total, and remaining which give the total number of items that need to be indexed as well as how many are left to be indexed.

hook_node_search_result

```
hook_node_search_result($node)
```

This hook is called when a search result is being returned for display. It is called after node_load and node_view have been called. You can use this hook to return additional information about a specific search result. You should return either a single string for display or an array of strings containing additional information. The information returned is stored in the extra property of the search results.

hook_node_update_index

```
hook_node_update_index($node)
```

This hook allows you to add additional information to a node during the indexing process. The hook is called after the node is both loaded and rendered using node_view. The results of the rendering process are stored in the $node->rendered property of the node. You should return either a single text string that you would like indexed by the system or an array of text that should be indexed by Drupal.

hook_ranking

```
hook_ranking()
```

This hook allows you to inform Drupal about factors that should be utilized when determining which order search results should be displayed in. These factors are then displayed to site administrators who change the weight of each factor or disable a factor completely to customize the search process for their site.

You should return an associative array that describes each ranking factor for your module. The array should contain the following keys:

- `title` — the name of the ranking algorithm for display to site administrators.
- `join` — a partial query string that can be used to join other tables to the base query. For example, you can use this to combine a table containing user ratings with the nodes they are rating. Tables should be joined to `i.sid`, which represents the search index item ID.
- `score` — a partial query string that is used to calculate the rank of a row within the database. The score should be a decimal value from 0 to 1.
- `arguments` — the arguments variable can be used to pass an array of data to the score query string. You can use this to pass the active user ID, the location of the user, maximum ranking for a voting algorithm, and so on.

Changed methods

In addition to the new hooks described above, several changes to the Search API have been made to add parameters making building forms easier:

- `search_box` — the `search_box` method has been modified to include the `$form_state` parameter, which holds the current state of the form including the current values of each form element. This makes it easier to render the search box in block form.
- `search_form` — the method is used to display a search form. It has been modified to include the `$form` parameter as the first parameter. This allows the form to be defined prior to this method being called which allows hooks to modify the search form more readily.

Removed methods

To facilitate some of the above changes, a few methods were removed from the Search API. These include:

- `do_search` — Drupal 7 now recommends that modules that would like to implement a search do so directly using DBTNG and the `SearchQuery` extension.
- `hook_search` — this hook was removed and split by operation into `hook_search_info`, `hook_search_admin`, `hook_search_execute`, `hook_search_reset`, and `hook_search_access`.

Cron changes

The cron system in Drupal has been modified to accommodate tasks that need to be run regularly, but that may not complete within a normal page load. This is accomplished using the `hook_cron_queue_info` hook. Cron also now ensures that cron is not canceled if the PHP time limit is reached while cron is executing.

hook_cron_queue_info

```
hook_cron_queue_info()
```

This hook allows you to define processes that need to be executed by Drupal in the background rather than being executed immediately during the cron run. To define these processes, you will create and return an associative array with the following values:

- `worker callback` — the callback that should be executed when the queue is run
- `time` — the maximum amount of time that should be spent executing the callback per cron run

The callback will receive an item definition that includes a unique `item_id`, the `time` the item was created, an `expire` key indicating the time when the item expires, and optionally, user `data` that can be added to the item.

You define the actual items that need to be processed including data for each item within `hook_cron`. This is done by getting an instance of a queue and then calling `createItem` on the queue for each item that needs to be processed. Let's take a look at a sample implementation that simply processes each node created after a specific time:

```php
<?php
function drupal7rocks_cron() {
  $last_time = variable_get('drupal7rocks_last_run_time', 0);
  $result = db_query("SELECT nid FROM {node}
   WHERE created > :created",
   array(':created' => $last_time,
  ));
  $queue = DrupalQueue::get('drupal7rocks_queue');
  foreach ($result as $nid) {
    $queue->createItem($nid);
  }
  variable_set('drupal7rocks_last_run_time', time());
}
?>
```

This implementation will load all nodes created since the last time cron was run and create an item for each node. The worker callback can then process each item to perform the needed business logic.

Tokens

The Token API has also had several new methods added to it to make creation of tokens easier as well as making it possible to change tokens defined by other modules. Let's look at each new method in detail.

hook_tokens

```
hook_tokens($type, $tokens, array $data = array(), array $options =
array())
```

This method is called to perform the actual translation of tokens from placeholders into the correct value for the text. The tokens array will contain a list of all tokens that were found in the source text. You should return an associative array with the values for each token that your module defines. For more information on translating tokens as well as the options available, see: `http://api.drupal.org/api/function/hook_tokens/7`.

hook_token_info

```
hook_token_info()
```

This hook is used to define information about the token types and specific tokens that are defined by a module. For more information on the format as well as examples, see:

`http://api.drupal.org/api/function/hook_token_info/7`.

hook_token_info_alter

```
hook_token_info_alter(&$data)
```

With this hook, you can change the tokens that have been defined by other modules.

token_info

```
token_info()
```

This method is used to get information about all of the tokens that exist within the system. An array is returned from the method with the name, description, and type of each token. Information about each type is also returned including the name of the type and the description of the type.

Image handling

To support the new image manipulation functionality, several new hooks have been added:

hook_image_default_styles

```
hook_image_default_styles()
```

You may implement this hook in your module to programmatically define image styles that can be used by your module or by other modules. You should only define additional styles if you cannot reuse the default styles provided by Drupal. You can also use this hook to move your image styles into code to make it easier to manage site changes.

hook_image_styles_alter

```
hook_image_styles_alter($styles)
```

When you implement this hook, you can change information about the styles defined by other modules. Please be careful when modifying styles to avoid users being frustrated by their changes not taking effect.

hook_image_style_delete

```
hook_image_style_delete($style)
```

This hook allows you to react when an image style is deleted within the system. A possible replacement name may be defined as $style['name']. This gives you the opportunity to reset any images that your module manages as needed.

hook_image_style_flush

```
hook_image_style_flush($style)
```

Drupal will call this hook when it detects that all images need to be regenerated from scratch. If your hook caches images after they have been manipulated, you should make sure to define this hook.

hook_image_style_save

```
hook_image_style_save($style)
```

This hook is called when image styles are changed within the system. If you are caching images, you should ensure that your module updates the cache when this hook is called.

hook_image_effect_info

```
hook_image_effect_info()
```

This hook returns additional information about custom image effects that are defined by a module. The image effects can then be used to manipulate images for display within the site. The hook should return an associative array with the following keys: label, effect callback, help, form callback, and summary theme.

hook_image_toolkits

```
hook_image_toolkits()
```

If you would like to define additional toolkits that can be used to process images, you can utilize this method to inform Drupal of the new toolkit. For more information on creating image toolkits, see the documentation at: http://api.drupal.org/api/function/hook_image_toolkits/7.

Trigger changes

The creation of triggers has become significantly easier in Drupal 7. To define a trigger that actions can respond to, you now simply need to implement `hook_trigger_info`. This hook should return an associative array of trigger information. The format of the array is as follows:

- module name — the key should be the name of the module that defines the trigger
- Hook name — the key of the next layer of the array is the name of the hook that describes the trigger
- The final layer of the array should have a single element that contains information on the label of the trigger

For more information, see the documentation at: `http://api.drupal.org/api/function/hook_trigger_info/7`.

RDF API

To support the new RDF functionality in Drupal 7, a new hook has been added to the Drupal API. The new hook is `hook_rdf_mapping`, which allows you to define RDF mappings for the field bundles attached to entities defined by the module. The return value of the method should be a nested array defining the structure of the mapping as follows:

- `type` — the entity name
- `bundle` — the name of the bundle (content type) that the mapping applies to
- `mapping` — an associative array with a key for each field to be mapped
- `predicates` — an array of RDF predicates describing the relationships between the bundle and the value of the field. The value will be text, another bundle, or a URL.
- `datatype` — a type used with the callback to format data so that it is readable by machines. For example, you can use this to properly format dates so that a computer can use the data.
- `callback` — a method to be called for the given datatype
- `type` — a string used in the RDFa markup to identify the type of the field
- `rdftype` — a property that is an array of RDF classes used to define the type of the instance

For more information on mapping fields, see: `http://api.drupal.org/api/function/hook_rdf_mapping/7`.

Translation API changes

To enhance the functionality for translating content into different languages, Drupal 7 has added several new hooks to allow your modules to interact with the translation system.

hook_language_fallback_candidates_alter

```
hook_language_fallback_candidates_alter(array
    &$fallback_candidates)
```

This hook allows you to control the order with which languages will be used for translation purposes if a translation for content is not available in the user's chosen language.

hook_language_negotiation_info

```
hook_language_negotiation_info()
```

Modules can use this hook to define language providers, which can be used to perform URL rewriting, translation, and more. For more information about defining language providers, see: http://api.drupal.org/api/function/hook_language_negotiation_info/7.

hook_language_negotiation_info_alter

```
hook_language_negotiation_info_alter(array
    &$language_providers)
```

Similar to other alter hooks, this hook allows you to change the language providers built by other modules.

hook_language_switch_links_alter

```
hook_language_switch_links_alter(array &$links, $type, $path)
```

This hook allows you to change the links that are used to change between languages. For example, you may re-translate the text of the link or point the link to a different destination. This method was called hook_translation_link_alter in Drupal 6.

hook_language_types_info

```
hook_language_types_info()
```

Using this hook, you can define additional languages that can be used within your Drupal site. You should return an associative array of languages where the key is the name of the language and the value is a description of the language.

hook_language_types_info_alter

```
hook_language_types_info_alter(array &$language_types)
```

This hook allows you to change or remove languages defined by other modules to give you additional control over the languages defined within your site.

hook_multilingual_settings_changed

```
hook_multilingual_settings_changed()
```

When changes are made to the language settings within Drupal, this hook will be called. This hook allows you to rebuild cached content as needed based on your module's business rules.

hook_node_prepare_translation

```
hook_node_prepare_translation($node)
```

This hook allows you to make a node ready to be translated. You can use this hook to load additional information that will be needed during the translation process.

Coder module

Although we have covered a wide range of changes to the Drupal API and there are many changes which could affect your modules, there is a solution to help make these changes more manageable. The Coder Module, which can be downloaded from: http://drupal.org/project/coder, automates many of the changes needed to conform with the new Drupal API.

When you want to upgrade your module to Drupal 7, it is highly recommended that you run your existing code through the coder module as a first step in the conversion process. This can help to minimize the amount of time you have to spend on the conversion.

Testing framework

Drupal 7 also introduces a new testing framework called SimpleTest that can be used to test the business logic of your modules. A full discussion of the testing process is beyond the scope of this book, but we will do a quick walkthrough of the framework and look at some of the hooks that your module may want to implement to interact with the SimpleTest framework. For a complete discussion of building tests using the SimpleTest framework, see: `http://drupal.org/simpletest`.

Setting up SimpleTest

To use SimpleTest, you need to do some configuration of your PHP installation.

- The CURL extension for PHP must be enabled.
- The DOM extension for PHP must be enabled. This should be done already in all installations of PHP 5.
- A `memory_limit` of at least 256 MB should be configured.
- SimpleTest must be enabled within the module manager. This is called Testing within the module manger.
- HTTP authentication settings for SimpleTest should be configured correctly for your server at `admin/config/development/simpletest/settings`. This is needed so that SimpleTest can accurately replicate.

After you have completed this initial configuration, you are ready to run tests.

Running tests

After the Testing module has been enabled, you can run tests by navigating to the test manager, which can be accessed within the configuration area of the administration interface, or by navigating directly to `admin/config/development/testing`.

The test interface appears as follows:

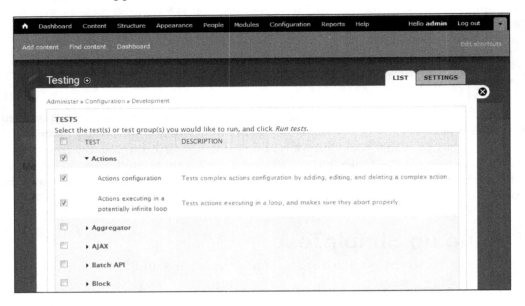

Simply select the tests you want to run and then click on **Run tests** at the bottom of the page.

After the tests are run, a report will be presented to you describing the results of the test.

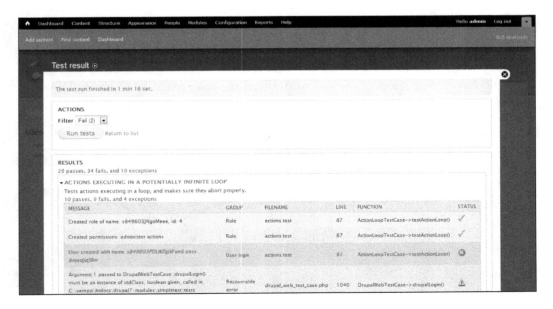

Creating Tests

To create a test for your module, we will create a PHP file that uses the naming convention, *modulename*.test where modulename is the name of your custom module. Within this file, you will create a class that inherits from `DrupalWebTestCase`. This class will allow you to create tests, set up your test case prior to running the tests, and clean up after the tests are run. Each test that you want to run will be created as a method starting with test. For example, if you wanted to test logging into the site, you may create a test called `testLogin`.

The `DrupalWebTestCase` class provides a large number of utility methods to perform common functionality needed within a test like logging in users, clicking on links, creating nodes, and so on. For more information on these utility methods, see: `http://drupal.org/node/265762`.

To ensure that your module performed correctly, you will use assertions. These allow you to test a variety of conditions within the site. If an assertion fails, the test will fail and you will know that you need to make a change to your module. The assertions that are available within SimpleTest are documented at: `http://drupal.org/node/265828`.

Available hooks

If you would like to interact with the test framework, you can utilize the following hooks:

hook_test_finished

```
hook_test_finished($results)
```

This hook is called when a single test has finished. The result of the test will be passed to the hook.

hook_test_group_started

```
hook_test_group_started()
```

This hook is called when testing of a specific test group has started.

hook_test_group_finished

```
hook_test_group_finished()
```

This hook is called when testing of a specific test group has completed.

hook_simpletest_alter

```
hook_simpletest_alter(&$groups)
```

This hook allows you to add or remove tests from a list of tests the user has selected to run. You can use this if your module overrides specific behavior of another module and would therefore cause those tests to fail.

Summary

In this chapter, we have reviewed many of the changes to the Drupal API including coverage of the methods which been added, changed, or removed from the API. Throughout the chapter, we have looked at the API in terms of upgrading your existing modules and site code to Drupal 7.

We have now reached the end of the book. I hope that you have enjoyed learning all about the new features and functionality that have been added to Drupal 7, and that you agree that Drupal 7 is a truly impressive release that will make your site easier to build, more powerful, and more secure.

You should now be well prepared to upgrade your Drupal 6 sites to Drupal 7 and begin building new sites with Drupal 7. For more information on building sites with Drupal 7, check out the official Drupal site at http://drupal.org or look at the other great books about Drupal from Packt Publishing at http://www. packtpub.com/drupal-books.

Index

K

key concepts, DBTNG
- connections 175-177
- drivers 174, 175
- queries 177
- statements 177

key features, Drupal 7
- added jQuery UI to core 18
- added Seven theme, for administrator 18
- administration toolbar 10, 11
- built-in automated cron functionality 16
- context information for messages 16
- Field API 14
- files support 15
- images support 15
- improved filter system 15
- improved installation 8, 9
- improved interface, for content creation 12
- improved interface, for content type creation 13
- improved node access system 20
- improved security 16
- new plugin manager, adding 17
- New Stark theme 19
- new test framework, adding 20, 21
- overlay administration 10, 11
- Queue API, adding 20
- RDF capabilities 21
- rewritten database layer 19
- Seven theme, for administrator 17
- themed information, allowed additional preprocessing 18

L

l() function 165

M

master/slave relationship 202
media section, configuration settings
- file system 113
- image styles 114
- image toolkit 114
menu_contextual_links method 219
menu_delete_links method 219
menu_execute_active_handler method 220

menu_get_active_menu_name method 221
menu_get_active_menu_names method 219
menu_get_custom_theme method 219
menu_get_names method 220
menu_get_router method 219
menu_links_clone method 219
menu_load_links method 219
menu_local_actions method 220
menu_local_tasks method 220
menu_main_menu method 220
menu_path_is_external method 221
menu_primary_links method 221
menu_reset_static_cache method 220
menu_router_build method 221
menu_secondary_links method 221
menu_secondary_menu method 220
menu_set_active_menu_name method 222
menu_set_active_menu_names method 220
menu_set_custom_theme method
- methods, menu system changes 220
menu system changes
- changed methods 220
- methods 219
- new hooks 218
- removed methods 221
menu_tree_all_data method 221
menu_tree_data method 221
menu_tree_page_data method 221
menu_valid_path method 222
merge statement syntax
- about 200
- creating 200
- example 200
methods
- addExpression 187
- addField 182
- addJoin 185
- addTag 196
- countQuery 186
- db_delete 201
- db_insert 197
- db_query 182
- db_query_range 179, 188
- db_select 182
- db_transaction 202
- db_update 199
- defaultOptions 181

U

update statement syntax
  about 199
  example 199
user management
  about 126
  account settings 126-129
  login rate limitations 130, 131
  password strength meter 130
  user fields 129
user_role_change_permissions method 239
user_role_grant_permissions method 239
user_role_permissions method 239
user_role_revoke_permissions method 239

V

values method 198
variable_set function 53

W

Web Services section, configuration settings
  about 118
  Feed aggregator 119
  RSS publishing 119
where method 192

X

XAMPP
  downloading 27

Z

ZIP files 209

Thank you for buying
Drupal 7 First Look

About Packt Publishing

Packt, pronounced 'packed', published its first book "*Mastering phpMyAdmin for Effective MySQL Management*" in April 2004 and subsequently continued to specialize in publishing highly focused books on specific technologies and solutions.

Our books and publications share the experiences of your fellow IT professionals in adapting and customizing today's systems, applications, and frameworks. Our solution based books give you the knowledge and power to customize the software and technologies you're using to get the job done. Packt books are more specific and less general than the IT books you have seen in the past. Our unique business model allows us to bring you more focused information, giving you more of what you need to know, and less of what you don't.

Packt is a modern, yet unique publishing company, which focuses on producing quality, cutting-edge books for communities of developers, administrators, and newbies alike. For more information, please visit our website: www.packtpub.com.

About Packt Open Source

In 2010, Packt launched two new brands, Packt Open Source and Packt Enterprise, in order to continue its focus on specialization. This book is part of the Packt Open Source brand, home to books published on software built around Open Source licences, and offering information to anybody from advanced developers to budding web designers. The Open Source brand also runs Packt's Open Source Royalty Scheme, by which Packt gives a royalty to each Open Source project about whose software a book is sold.

Writing for Packt

We welcome all inquiries from people who are interested in authoring. Book proposals should be sent to author@packtpub.com. If your book idea is still at an early stage and you would like to discuss it first before writing a formal book proposal, contact us; one of our commissioning editors will get in touch with you.

We're not just looking for published authors; if you have strong technical skills but no writing experience, our experienced editors can help you develop a writing career, or simply get some additional reward for your expertise.

Drupal 7

ISBN: 978-1-84951-286-2   Paperback: 416 pages

A comprehensive beginner's guide to installing, configuring, and building a professional Drupal 7 website

1. Set up, configure, and deploy a Drupal 7 website

2. Easily add exciting and powerful features

3. Design and implement your website's look and feel

4. Promote, manage, and maintain your live website

Drupal Web Services

ISBN: 978-1-84951-098-1   Paperback: 304 pages

Integrate social and multimedia Web services and applications with your Drupal Web site.

1. Explore different Web services and how they integrate with the Drupal CMS.

2. Reuse the applications without coding them again using the Web services protocols on your Drupal site.

3. Configure your Drupal site to consume various web services by using contributed Drupal modules for each specific task or application.

4. Packed with hands-on-examples, case studies, and clear explanations for better understanding

Please check **www.PacktPub.com** for information on our titles

www.ingramcontent.com/pod-product-compliance
Lightning Source LLC
Chambersburg PA
CBHW060522060326
40690CB00017B/3351